A Death on the Barrens

George James Grinnell

For Chris Mack

Best wishes

George Grinnell

Published 1996 by
Northern Books
P. O. Box 211, Station P
Toronto, Ontario
M5S 2S7

First Printing: January, 1996

Canadian Cataloguing in Publication Data
Grinnell, George James, 1933-
A death on the barrens

Includes bibliographical references.
ISBN 0-96804040-3
I. Northwest, Canadian — Description and travel. 2.
Philosophy
of nature — Canada. I. Title.
FC3963.G74 1996   917.1904'3   C95-950328-5
F1060.92.G74 1996

Cover design, and layout
steve long's Graphic Solutions
Port Hawkesbury, Nova Scotia

Front cover photo by Keith McLarnen
Back cover photo by Bob Martin

Printed and bound in Canada
Strait Printing, Port Hawkesbury, Nova Scotia

Dedication

This book is dedicated to the memory of my father, George Morton Grinnell (1902-1953), and to the memory of the leader of the expedition across the Barren Grounds of Keewatin, Arthur Moffatt (1919-1955), and to the memory of Sandy Host (1954-1984), Betty Eamer (1961-1984), George Landon Grinnell (1962-1984), and Andrew Preble Grinnell (1968-1984), who died together on the barren coast of James Bay.

History
is the attempt
to write a transcendental piece of music
and then
by our own free will
to play it.

Laurie

A Death on the Barrens

Part II: August

Part III: September

Epilogue

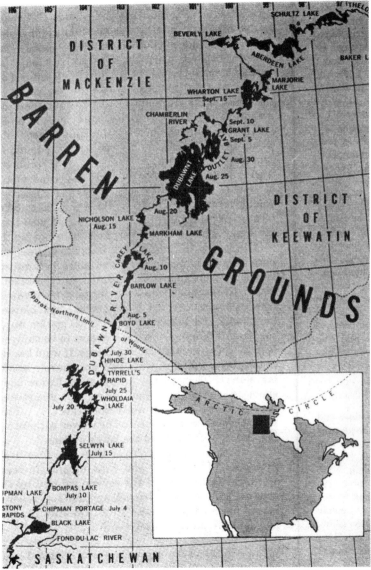

photo credit Sports Illustrated

i

photo credit Skip Pessl

Arthur Moffatt (1919-1955)
on his final expedition.

Introduction

On September 14, 1955, Art Moffatt, an experienced wilderness canoeist, died from exposure on the banks of the Dubawnt River, deep in the heart of the Barren Lands of northern Canada. He was thirty-six. The five younger companions with him just barely survived.

After forty years of reflection, guilt, and gestation, this book represents the personal story of that unusual wilderness sojurn and that horrific day by one of its survivors. Intertwined and juxtaposed, it is also a tale of George Grinnell's travels through life. Both tales are unconventional and fascinating.

The 1955 canoe story can be viewed from either of two extreme perspectives. The first view is the practical and dismissive observation that as a remote sub-arctic canoe expedition it was poorly planned and irresponsibly executed, and that its tragic conclusion was a natural consequence of that folly. It is, however, a truthful story about a real canoe trip, with all its associated petty human interactions and problems. Many of the trip's problems arise from the gnawing reality of incessant hunger, resulting from an inadequate daily food ration.

Most individuals who have travelled in the Barrens have been affected by them in some spiritual manner. My first canoe venture into the Barrens was also on the Dubawnt, in 1969. Due to the late ice that year and similar food shortages, it was a hard trip. But it affected me deeply and I have returned five times since then, to do similar crossings of the Barrens in the same area, trying to recapture that same spiritual experience. It is precisely this vivid spiritual experience that permeates George's narrative and makes it a joy to read.

In the words of the author: "the real voyage is travelled within one's soul." And as a spiritual odyssey it was a truly extraordinary passage.

The majority of us live our lives in relative psychological security, choosing to graze in the center of the pastures of the human asylum. We leave it to genuine artists and individuals, like George Grinnell, to explore the unseen and less traveled edges of our enclosure for us. This exploration of the human soul is far more difficult than any exploration of the geographical landscape can possibly be. It is both difficult to arrive at the edge, the place of enlightenment, of heightened sensation and perception, and then equally difficult to return and to re-attach to the humdrum everyday world of the center.

Their three-month canoe trip across the uninhabited Barrens takes George Grinnell to the lip of the abyss that separates sanity from insanity and life from death. And it is his first hand exploration of this uncertain edge that provides the profound insights that makes this a most powerful and unique narrative.

To illustrate with just one such exploration in *A Death on the Barrens*: in chapter sixteen, the author describes his experience of a temporary loss of identity and the associated panic attack. He was in terror that his soul was being "vaporized by the wilderness" — by an overwhelming wilderness that lives forever, and one that cares not a whit about a human individual. The *nothingness* of the barrenland wilderness was almost too much for the youthful psyche to bear.

Edward McCourt, in his book *The Yukon and the Northwest Territories*, asks the rhetorical question: "Why do men go to the Barren Lands?"

In an eloquent passage, a portion of which follows, he answers: "... the Barren Grounds is a world so vast, so old, so remote from common experience as to encourage the annihilation of self; its sheer immensity reduces the individual by comparison to a bubble on the surface of a great river, a foam-fleck on the ocean; and its great age — its rocks are the oldest in the world — shrinks his life-span to unmeasurable minuteness. It is a world which affords so little evidence of man's existence that it tends to suspend the passions we associate most commonly with him — love, hate, pride, fear. And in the long run it makes what a man does or does not do seem of little moment, even to himself. It is a world which by reason of its seeming invulnerability challenges the brash, optimistic young to attempt great things and assures the old that what they have failed to do makes no difference."

Arthur Moffatt's Grave at Baker Lake N.W. T.
after R.C.M.P. recovered the body.

Chapter One
The Mounties

Before our food arrived that afternoon, we four divided up the sugar bowl between us and drank the contents of the cream pitcher. The following morning, the manager of Churchill, Manitoba's one hotel told us the Mounties wanted to see us. As we walked up the frozen dirt street to RCMP headquarters, snow swirled about in the wind. I saw a crust of bread in the dirt and reached for it, as did the others. We laughed at our good fortune. Our bellies were full now, full to the point of bursting; but the sensation of being hungry had not left, and we could not stop eating, nor saving food. To be on the safe side, I put the crust in my pocket, even though my companions and I had already filled our hotel rooms with food.

Our hands and feet had not yet thawed out. Another three months would pass before the yellow swelling would return to a more normal shape, or feeling would return to our toes, or the black marks of frostbite on our fingers would flush once again to a healthy tone of pink; but we were safe now and happy, and so we smiled and laughed a lot.

The Mounties divided us up into separate rooms and asked us to tell of the events which had led to the death of our leader, Arthur Moffatt. The young Mountie who interviewed me was friendly and encouraging as I spoke. At the end, he concluded: "So you lost your sense of reality."

I stared at him in uncomprehending disbelief. Perhaps it is true that back in June, when I had first joined the others at Stony Rapids, a Hudson's Bay post on Lake Athabaska, I had not had a very profound appreciation of reality. I had had visions of heroic deeds and epic accomplishments. I had been on my best behavior. But the luxury of my youthful illusions had been stripped from me soon enough.

My first awareness of Reality with a capital "R" came to me in the form of hunger, that everlasting hunger that must be satisfied or death will in time arrive; and my second awareness came in the form of freezing cold, which kills more quickly. In the face of this awareness, the real me — a vulnerable, petty, selfish, greedy, cowardly me — surfaced. Despite my best intentions, by the time Art died, I had no more control over my actions than he had over his. I lived, he died: that is all I have to say. What more reality must I be burdened with?

I felt as if Art had given us all a great gift. The day he lay frozen on the tundra and I sat beside him in the sunlight, I felt a warm spiritual peace envelop me like the grace of God. I had come to understand that life is good. I was grateful for the sunlight which warmed us and thawed our ice-coated clothing, grateful that it was his body which lay frozen on the

2

cold Tundra beside me and not my own. Reality had never seemed so sweet. Death would come when it would come — to us as to every living creature — as it had already come to Art. I felt grateful to the caribou we had shot, to the ptarmigan we had knifed, to the fish we had boiled into soup.

By the end of the trip, we loved one another as we had never loved before, because outside that perimeter of love was terror. We loved Peter when he brought back a fish. We loved Joe when he returned with a sack of driftwood, and we loved everyone else when we shared warmth as we shivered together in the night.

Art had brought us to reality. We ate, drank and breathed that reality night and day. We smelled that reality; we basked in the beauty of that reality; we studied the reality of the wilderness sky and the reality of the wilderness river; we shuddered in the fear of that reality. How graciously it fed us; how quickly it had killed Art. And so we huddled together in our spiritual cocoon of love, and lived in beauty frightened to death.

Acknowledging my cowardice, my pettiness, my greed in exchange for the gift of life seemed a small enough price to pay, to say nothing of the gift of love by which the others sheltered me from the terrifying abyss. Must I now face that other, more civilized, reality that no one could love a coward like me?

Art had stripped away all the protective structures of civilization so that we had no other defence against the awesome power of the wilderness, and we bathed in that love night and day.

Like Lord Jim in Joseph Conrad's tale, I had always believed that at the moment of truth, I would have performed the heroic rather than the cowardly act; but I found when faced with reality, I mean "Reality" (not some philosophical exercise in semantics during a course in English literature), dying that heroic death had little appeal. Like Lord Jim, I had saved myself.

My name is "Jim." My full name is George James Grinnell, but my father's name was George Morton Grinnell, and my great-uncle's was George Bird Grinnell, and his father's, George Blake Grinnell, and his father's, George Grinnell: and so, to give me an identity in a family full of "Georges," they called me "Jim," and Jim I turned out to be, like Lord Jim, a coward, so if you don't mind, for now, just call me, "George."

The Mountie stared at me.
I stared at the Mountie.
He smiled at me.

Perhaps, during the course of my tale, he had developed a certain amount of sympathy for me and was hinting that a plea of insanity, or a "loss of a sense of reality," might not be viewed unfavorably by the civilized authorities.

Chapter Two
Embarkation

A quarter of a year earlier, when I had arrived at Stony Rapids and had joined Art and the others in a small shack that had been built for the pilots when their DC-3 was unable to return to civilization for whatever reason, I had fallen in love with Art as had everyone else, but it was a different sort of love then than I felt at the end of the trip. Every time Art stood up to go outside, I would stand up and follow him. I laughed at his jokes and memorized his words. We all loved Art in those early days as if he were not the leader of an expedition, but of a religious cult and we his five anointed disciples.

Skip Pessl, the number one disciple and second-in-command, commented on how well we were all getting on.

"Enjoy it while it lasts," Art replied.

Like the others, I had laughed at Art's cynicism, for I was convinced "it" would last for ever. I was eager to get away from civilization and to escape from those former personal relationships which had brought me so much pain. I had a feeling that on this expedition I would be able to start life over again, leave my old self behind. I was determined to stop rebelling against everybody and everything, which I believed had contributed to the death of my father; no more speeches on the corner of Wall Street and Broad denouncing the capitalist system; no more getting myself thrown out of Harvard; no more summary courts martial for disrespect to my commanding officer.

The prospect of becoming the new me, a person everyone would like and admire, was exciting. I was full of eager anticipation like a child before a birthday party, my own birthday party. I was about to be born again, strong, courageous, heroic, self-sacrificing, obliging, witty: in general, the most loveable person in the world. I felt like a caterpillar anticipating its miraculous transmutation into a butterfly. In those early days of the trip, I just smiled and followed Art around. I was happy for the first time since my father had died two years earlier. I had found a new father.

Art had been on six previous trips into the wilderness, and before that had served with the American Field Service assigned to the British Eighth Army in Africa for three years; he, therefore, had met Reality before. But Joe Lannouette and Bruce LeFavour, my fellow bowmen and novices like me, had been brought up in civilization and had felt as I felt, that some protective veil would always hang between us and the Abyss. All three of us followed Art around looking for guidance, trying to pick up words of wisdom, seeking to be born again. In those early days we were all so very obliging.

Four days later, when we left Stony Rapids and headed into the wilderness, Art took over the job of cooking dinner and of passing out the luncheon rations, while Frederick "Skip" Pessl, as second-in-command, was given the job of cooking breakfast. Bruce, who liked to cook, volunteered for the job; but Art declined his offer.

"He who controls the food, controls the men," Art said with a wry smile that curled up the left side of his mouth while the right side held firm.

We all laughed, as we had laughed at his other bits of wisdom. In those early days, I was glad he was in control of the food. I trusted his judgment more than Bruce's, more even than my own. Art seemed so wise. He was fifteen years older than I, more realistic and more experienced in all things.

Skip Pessl, the second-in-command, and I were the same age, twenty-two. Joe Lanouette, Art's bowman, was twenty; Peter Franck, my sternman, was nineteen, and so was Bruce LeFavour, Skip's bowman. Art was thirty-six, old enough to be more experienced and more wise, but not so much older as to be out of touch with our youthful longing for adventure.

I had been in the American Army the previous February when I had received Art's letter. He had wanted to know if I would join him, Peter Franck, and Skip Pessl on an expedition by canoe across the Barren Grounds of sub-Arctic Canada. The Barrens had been crossed by two other expeditions involving white men: Hearne in 1772, in the company of Chipewyan Indians; and the Tyrrell brothers in 1893, accompanied by Iroquois. We would be the first all non-native expedition to attempt it.

I had not known Art before the expedition, but he lived at the end of the same dirt road in Norwich, Vermont, where Lewis Teague, a painter, lived. Lewis had once been married to my cousin, but was divorced and remarried to a beautiful woman named Virginia, with whom I was in love (in yet another meaning of the word "love"). It was Lewis Teague who had given Art my name as an ideal candidate for a long distance canoe trip into the frozen Arctic.

Bruce and Joe joined the expedition later, to bring our numbers up from four to six.

My discharge from the Army was slow in coming because earlier in the year I had been court martialled; and I did not arrive at Stony Rapids, Saskatchewan, till the 27th of June, about two weeks later than Art had originally planned to embark. The others had been waiting for me about a week, but we had not headed into the wilderness immediately. Earlier that Spring, a barge that supplies the communities on Lake Athabaska had brought our canoes and other equipment; but our food had been left off the manifest, and Art had had to scrounge a three months supply from the Hudson's Bay Post and from a private trader. He was able to fill the canoes to the gunwales, but the makeshift supplies were heavy; and the only case of peanut butter available was in glass jars. Art preferred unbreakable plastic containers for obvious reasons. He had radioed out to civilization, but the case of peanut butter in plastic jars did not arrive on my flight, nor on the next plane, which arrived two days later; and so, after too many

8

delays, we loaded our ton of food and equipment onto Stony Rapids' one truck and headed up the rapids on Stony Rapids' one road to Black Lake with our peanut butter still in glass jars.

Trollenberg, the driver, thought that our supplies were too heavy for his one-ton truck. Art said that he could not afford to pay for two trips; we would have to walk. Trollenberg relented, but his truck experienced difficulties even in low gear. He stopped frequently to let the engine cool and to top up the radiator with water. The supplies which were too heavy for his truck would be the supplies which would be too heavy for our backs as we portaged and paddled up to the Height of Land and then canoed down the other side towards the Arctic Circle. Our progress was slow by truck, and it was soon to become a great deal slower when we came to the end of the road.

At the fishing camp at Black Lake, as we stowed away boxes and packs, the large "prospector" model canoes from the Chestnut Canoe Company lay low in the water. The canoes became very stable, so stable we could walk along the gunwales without tipping them over. We soon discovered that the cause of this amazing stability was owing not just to the weight of the loads, but to the fact that the canoes had come to rest at the bottom of the lake. Small waves sloshed over the gunwales.

As we headed out from shore, we wondered what we had forgotten. Matches? Spare paddles?

"Are the spare paddles in your canoe, Skip?" Art asked. There was a pause.

We debated whether to continue without them or to go back. Art decided to make camp; but by the time we had recovered the paddles from the Hudson's Bay warehouse next day, the wind had started to blow. Our canoes, with two inches of freeboard, began to swamp; and so we were forced back to the same campsite for another couple of days.

Summers tend to be short in the Arctic. The ice leaves the lakes in July, if at all, and returns shortly thereafter; and the wind blows fiercely for days on end until the wintry blizzards cover the tundra in snow and ice.

"If I were superstitious," Skip commented, "I would almost believe we were not meant to go down the Dubawnt."

"Don't worry," Art replied. "We've got all summer."

We laughed and repeated the joke several times during the next few days while the wind blew.

Art put a brave face on our situation, but inwardly he was not laughing.

"I felt sad, apprehensive, and gloomy," Art wrote on the eve of our adventure, while the rest of us followed him around with smiles on our faces, believing he would carry us through all adversity.

On the evening of the second day, the wind calmed, and we embarked in the middle of the night. It was a lovely evening with the sun glowing pink over the northern horizon. I looked across the lake to the far shore and thought I saw the lights of houses as if I were looking across Long Island Sound, or over some benign rural lake in cottage country far to the south; but there were no lights across the lake, nor any people. Before another human being would cross our path, a quarter of a year would pass, Art would be dead, and those human beings would be speaking a language incomprehensible to us, the language of the Innuit.

Art dreamed that there was a toll at the end of the lake which he could not afford to pay.

It took us a week to complete the first major portage up the Chipman River out of Black Lake. At the end of the week, I was happy to have severed our last contact with civilization. I reflected with pleasure on our autonomy. We were now a law unto ourselves. We carried no radio. No one would know where we were, nor could they check up on what we did. It had seemed to me then that we were free to create our own reality, shape our own laws, live beyond the constraints of civilization: but I reflected upon such matters in the abstract only. During those early days of the trip, I was on my best behavior. I loved everyone, and I worshipped Art. He was more than my leader. He was my teacher, my role model, my spiritual guru, my father. He was the one I wanted to follow to the end of the Earth.

Art carried an aging wind-up pocket watch that did not tell very accurate time, but because we carried no radio, we were unable to synchronize our watches to the Central Standard Time on which civilization to the south hung its schedules; and so, as we headed into the wilderness, for lack of any more reliable frame of reference, we set our watches to agree with his. "Moffatt Time," we called it.

*George Grinnell, Bruce Lefavour and Skip Pessl
unloading the canoes for portage up the Chipman River.*

Chapter Three
Art Moffatt

During the first month of the voyage, I had three dreams about Art. In my first dream, he was dressed as a sergeant in the Army, which was not surprising, because (having just been discharged from the Army) I was still dressed in Army clothes myself. I still thought like a soldier, and I felt towards Art in real life much as I had felt towards the sergeants I had met in the Army; they were older and wiser, and I had respected them.

After I had fallen in love with Virginia Teague, I had felt I had no place to escape to but the Army, despite the fact that I considered myself to be an anti-war protestor at the time — or, at any rate, I did not want to get myself killed. The Korean "conflict" was on, and so I spent my early days in the Army explaining the merits of pacifism to my fellow soldiers, until a sergeant took me aside one day and told me gently that preaching pacifism was quite unnecessary in the Army. "In the Army," he said, "we are all pacifists."

This came as a revelation to me. Hitherto I thought soldiers enjoyed getting their parts blown off by land mines or other weapons of personal destruction, and therefore were always eager for war; but this particular sergeant had joined the Army in the depression because there were no other jobs available, and had ended up on Corregidor shortly before it was overrun by the Japanese. Like Art and other veterans, his experience in the war had confirmed his desire for peace.

I had looked into my sergeant's eyes and saw that he spoke the truth. What I found in the Army were not soldiers who liked to fight, but soldiers who liked to eat. The Army fed them at a time when jobs were hard to come by. Throughout history, jobs have frequently been hard to come by, especially if one is a young man with no clear track through the rat race.

The revelation that no one in the Army wanted to be there made me feel guilty about my own cowardice and about my past attempts to dodge the draft, so I volunteered for combat in Korea. The sergeant at headquarters tore up my application and threw me out of the orderly room and told me that if I came around again he would give me a "section eight" (that is to say, a discharge on grounds of mental instability).

What the old sergeants taught me were two things: "don't bug out, and don't volunteer." If you "bug out" (desert under fire), you leave your buddies to die. If you "volunteer," you will probably die yourself. The morality of my sergeants began and ended with concern for the lives of the young men closest to them. To survive, we had to obey; but our job was not to get ourselves killed unnecessarily. The old sergeants were like fathers to me, and I wanted Art to play that role, so I dreamed of him as a sergeant; but the image did not entirely fit. Art did not dress like a sergeant, he did not give orders, and he did not seem to acknowledge any militaristic chain of command.

When I had looked into Art's eyes, I had seen the same thing as in the eyes of that sergeant who had been captured by the Japanese at Corregidor: compassion for the foolishness of my youth, stoical resignation at the destructive proclivities of civilization, and (in the depths of his soul) a sanctuary of inner peace. But sergeants, however wise they may have been, gave orders. "You ain't being paid to think, soldier," they had repeatedly reminded me: and Art never gave orders.

During the Second World War, as a professed pacifist from America and a volunteer with the American Field Service, a Quaker organization, Art had been allowed by the British High Command to carry no weapons, just the wounded and dying soldiers back from the front; but after a short while, he had become convinced that the Second World War was total madness. His sympathies had fallen to the desert Arabs who were being overrun by both the British and the German Empires. From the Arab point of view, there was not much to choose between one Western Empire and the next: and Art had come to share their point of view. By the end of the war, he had quite enough of the British ideal of Empire and dreamed instead of returning to the peace of the wilderness, where there were no military hierarchies nor wars.

From day to day, we waited; and when Art stood up, we all stood up. When he struck his tent, we all struck our tents. When he loaded his canoe, we all loaded our canoes; but he never told us what to do, as a sergeant would have done.

In the Army, sergeants during combat are expected to know the whereabouts of their men at all times. If they do not know, either the absent man is shot for desertion, or the sergeant is court martialled for dereliction of duty; but Art did not seem to care where we were or what we were doing.

Early in the trip, when we were held up by the wind for two days, I had checked in with Art to see if he would give me permission to go for a walk while we waited. He was sitting on a rock staring at the waves on the lake, his back to me. "I don't care what you do," he said without turning around.

I felt hurt. Finally, he turned around and said in a more friendly voice, "Be back when the wind dies;" and then he smiled at me. I smiled back and turned and headed into the forest, but I never asked him again for permission to do anything; I just went ahead and did it, and the image of Art as a sergeant soon faded from my dream world. Nevertheless, if he did not seem to care what we did, and we were all perfectly free to do whatever we liked, there remained that one lingering restriction by which he maintained subtle influence.

"He who controls the food, controls the men," rings in my ears to this day. He cooked supper.

Art had not just repudiated war, he had repudiated the entire hierarchical structure of Western Civilization, whether it took the form of the military chain of command, the industrial-military complex, or a hypocritical church. In the wilderness, he recognized only one authority: the wind, or whatever forces of nature happened to be buffeting him at the moment.

We learned to watch and to wait; we did not obey, we imitated. But I was never quite sure who or what I was imitating; and as the trip wore on, I also began to wonder about the wisdom of a blind imitation of my peaceful guru who had surrendered to the wilderness, and my dream image of Art changed. In the new dream, he retained a position of authority over me, but my feelings towards that authority became alien.

Before we had been out of Stony Rapids ten days, Art had declared a holiday to rest. In those early days of the trip, we had been in poor shape. The black flies had eaten us alive during the day, and the mosquitoes at night. Although we were far behind schedule right from the beginning, we welcomed the holiday. It had seemed good that we were on our way at last.

At dinner, Bruce LeFavour had opened the conversation by asking what we thought the greatest adventure of all time had been. It was an interesting topic to us in those early days, before reality had raised our consciousness to other things. In those days, we were all measuring our adventure against the World's best, and we wanted to think of ourselves as heroes.

Bruce had first directed his question to Joe Lanouette, his former roommate at Dartmouth College, who had not wanted to come on the trip. Joe had been talked into volunteering by Bruce and had spent the previous week swearing at the black flies, at the heavy loads, and at Bruce; but now that we were resting on a rocky ledge by the lake, and the wind was blowing the bugs away, and Joe was seated comfortably on a rock sipping his tea and smoking a cigarette, he warmed to the subject and pontificated on the merits of the British expedition which had recently "conquered" Mount Everest.

Bruce nodded his head vigorously as if to encourage Joe. Bruce's father had been a newspaper executive, and Bruce had picked up some tricks on how to conduct a successful interview. He rarely expressed an opinion of his own, but always supported with nods and encouraging words whatever his interviewee was saying.

When Joe was finished speaking, Bruce had turned to Skip Pessl, the noble second-in-command. Skip was the sternman in Bruce's canoe, and they shared the same Army surplus mountain tent. As Skip spoke, Bruce nodded even more vigorously than he had when Joe had spoken, as perhaps befitted Skip's elevated status. Skip proved more knowledgeable than Joe about the "assault" and about previous failed attempts to "conquer" Everest.

Art remained silent, which was not unusual; but eventually Bruce brought him into the conversation by asking him directly what he thought. Art sipped his tea and said quietly that he preferred the way the Sherpas had learned to live in harmony with the mountains to the way the British had learned to plant flags on them.

After Art had spoken, the sentiments expressed around the campfire immediately changed. How ridiculous to "assault" a mountain! How pretentious to plant a flag! How arrogant to stand on top for fifteen minutes and talk of "conquest!" Skip tripped over himself trying to reverse his previous opinion, so as to agree with Art, while Joe stood his ground and looked sullen.

The long portage up to the Height of Land dragged on for weeks. The North is a country for young men, and Art suffered more than the rest of us. Art was of slight build, and the packs and boxes weighed heavily on his thin frame. Physically at thirty-six, he had passed through the vigor of his youth into the downward slide of middle age. While we grew stronger with every passing mile, Art grew more tired. He never complained, but his diary spoke of exhaustion.

> July 4th: ... The tump pulling on my neck was too much to take for more than 100 yards at a time. To take the strain off my neck I would

19

pull on the sides, at my ears, with my hands —
this made my arms so stiff at the elbows I
couldn't straighten them out. To rest, I had to
find a rock high enough to set the box on. I
could never have got it up by myself....
George and Pete each made two trips while I
was doing my one. Iron men. George never
rests. Good man. Joe says he found saying 'son
of a bitch, son of a bitch' at every step helped for
a while. But the flies are terrible....

Art was the smallest man on the expedition, but
he carried the heaviest load, which contained his
camera and nine thousand feet of film. He rarely
spoke. I misunderstood his silence for Stoicism. I
wanted him to be the father who could pick me up
and carry me on his shoulders, along with his other
loads, if I fell. I did not understand the other half of
the equation.

Art was worried, worried about his children, his
wife, the financial success of the expedition, worried
about his own stamina in the face of the gruelling
physical punishment the wilderness was meting out
to him. Outwardly, Art put a brave face on his plight;
but inwardly, his diary told a different story. "Can't
recapture confident, carefree air of first Albany trip
in 1937," he wrote.

As we sat by the campfire in the evening, I had
the naive idea that he would have been insulted had
I offered to help him carry his heavy camera chest;
and so I did not volunteer. Instead, I regaled him
with my philosophy of life, which I thought would

impress him: my youthful sense of liberation and power, my desire to live life to the fullest. Art nodded his head in an absent-minded sort of way before nodding off in the warmth of the fire.

> July 8th: ... Spent morning sewing up pants, burned night before while discussing philosophy with George.

When he was seventeen, Art had put a canoe on the Canadian National Railroad and had disembarked at Sioux Lookout, headwaters of the Albany River. The Albany was the longest wilderness river in Ontario, and Art had descended it alone, scared to death the whole time, as he said; but it was a different quality of fear than the fear he felt among the roar of cannons. The wilderness fear was a fear elevated by beauty into inner peace. The fear during battles was just fear degenerated into horror.

At the outposts along the way, the Indian women had been kind to Art, and he had not forgotten their kindness. During the War, he had drowned out the sound of cannons with the dream of this peaceful wilderness.

Before joining the America Field Service and the British Army, Art had attended Dartmouth College in Hanover, New Hampshire. Dartmouth prides itself on giving scholarships to Indians, and its students romp through the White Mountains with packs and tents on their backs. Art was small and slightly built; he was also an outsider.

Most of the students at Dartmouth were rich, but Art came from a humble background. His father looked after the horses of a wealthy homosexual who lived on Long Island, not far from where my grandmother had her summer place. The homosexual had had no children: and because Art had been born and raised on his estate, he had adopted Art as a surrogate son, paying his tuition at Dartmouth and leaving him a small inheritance, which Art ultimately used to purchase the little house where he and his wife and two daughters lived at the end of that dirt road in Norwich, Vermont. Thus, during his years at Dartmouth, Art did not fit in. Physically, he was no match for the other Dartmouth men; and socially, his background was not "comme il faut."

His wilderness trip down the Albany river at seventeen was an attempt to prove to himself, if not to his "chubber" Dartmouth colleagues, that he was "un homme de fer du nord:" as he said with an ironic laugh, "an iron man of the North." But what he had found instead was the warm sympathy of the Cree women, living in their simple villages along the river. They also adopted Art, for Art's mother had died when he was three: and Art adopted them. The Cree villages seemed so natural to him, in comparison with his heritage on the wealthy estates of Long Island, where he both did and did not belong as heir and stable boy rolled into one. He was grateful to his wealthy benefactor, of whom he always spoke with respect: but he loved the Cree.

After the War, he took Carol, his new bride, down the Albany to meet the Cree; and when Carol produced their first child, they named her "Creigh," after a friend of Carol's. But "Creigh" is pronounced "Cree," and Art always said the name with a smile. Art's pride and joy was a Moosehide jacket the Cree women had sewn for him.

Art attempted to earn a living guiding young men down the Albany to these Cree villages. With an old movie camera loaned by a neighbor, Art made a movie of the Albany River. In the winter, he toured around giving lectures about the Cree way of life, but there was not much money in it; and although his benefactor had left him enough to buy a house, there was not enough additional funding to support a family. Art decided to head further north into the Barren Grounds.

He bought a new camera and nine thousand feet of film, and moved off with us across the largest uninhabited land in North America, hoping to earn a living as a wildlife photographer; but making a film was not his true vocation. The wilderness called him in other ways.

As the days passed into weeks, we burned off the fatty lining from our oesophagi so that we felt hungry before, after, and during meals. The hunger began to express itself at dinner with a friendly rivalry to be first in line, and was soon accompanied by an intense concentration as we dipped the doling cup through the "glop."

"Glop" consisted of two boxes of Catelli macaroni, which Art had scrounged out of the storehouse of the Hudson's Bay Post at Stony Rapids; two tins of tomato paste; two packages of dehydrated soup; and two cans of "Spork" or "Spam" — all boiled up in a gallon or two of water. The water was free and Art made the most of it.

The food was not elegant, but we loved Art's glops. The hungrier we became, the more we loved them. Particularly we loved the fatty Spork and Spam. On the portages, we were burning up about twice as many calories as we were getting from our rations. The more calories we burned, the more we craved food, especially fatty foods. Art cut up the Spork and Spam in small pieces and stirred them in well, but not all pieces were the same size. By being first in line for dinner, we had a better opportunity for snaring bigger and fattier pieces.

Young, wiry, and nervous, Peter Franck was in the habit of darting the doling cup artfully along the surface; but the technique of husky Joe Lanouette was much more successful. He dipped the doling cup deep into the pot, moving it slowly, ever so slowly, along the bottom. A sure hand, he always seemed to come up with the most desired morsels.

While Peter Franck was almost always first over the portages and Joe Lanouette almost always last, Joe came alive at feeding time and could generally beat Peter and the rest of us to the head of the line. He also seemed to have an iron mouth and could gulp down his first bowl in record speed, so as to be first in line for seconds as well; but he was by no means the only one to rush.

For the first time in my life, I had experienced the reality of hunger, the long-term, gnawing reality of hunger that reminded me that my life depended on things beyond my control. We six had broken our dependency on civilization, and now my hunger reminded me of my dependency on Art. When the last item was eaten out of the bottom of our canoes, what then, Art?

As we travelled deeper into the wilderness, my rush to the glop pot became ever more intense. The only men who did not rush for the glop were Art and Skip, our leaders. Art did not rush because he always helped himself first before calling us to dinner. He ate out of a larger bowl than the rest of us. Skip, the second-in-command, did not rush because he was a man of high principles. While the rest of us laughed and joked about who had captured the fattiest morsels, Skip ate dinner silently and scowled.

After about two weeks, when it became clear to everyone that Skip did not approve of our dinner manners, Bruce Lefavour, Skip's bowman and tentmate, decided to follow Skip's noble example. One evening, when Joe, Pete and I rushed for the pot, Bruce and Skip out-did each other in their politeness. Finally, they both stopped and did the gentlemanly "after-you-Alphonse" routine. Skip finally insisted, as second-in-command, that Bruce stand in line in front of him.

That evening Joe Lanouette emitted an horrendous belch as he hurried to be first in line for "seconds." This was too much for Skip. "Just because we are living in the wilderness," he scolded, "doesn't mean we have to act like savages."

Silence fell. The word "savages," rang in our ears. Skip had just denigrated "savages" by comparing them to us. Art worshipped the so-called "savages." No one said anything for a long time. Finally, Art managed a discreet, but audible, belch of disapproval. We laughed, all except Skip, whose face turned various shades of purple before looking apologetically over to Art. Art smiled at him, and Skip smiled at Art; but beneath the surface, their attitudes towards "savages," the conquest of nature, and leadership were all very different. As the days passed into weeks, these differences began to surface with ever-increasing frequency.

Early in the trip, I had traded my ration of chocolate bars, which Art sometimes distributed at lunch, for paper to write on. Our monetary system was now based solely on food. Although we all had contributed $200 equally towards the cost of the expedition's food, control of that food, that wealth, had been taken over by Art and by Skip.

By the end of the second week, my dream image of Art had changed from sergeant to that of a wealthy banker dressed in formal evening wear, welcoming a multitude of five thousand hungry guests at a great banquet on a mossy, rock-bestrewn hillside in the wilderness serving "glop." I still saw Art as the man in authority, but it was no longer the authority of a sergeant in the Army: instead, it was the authority of wealth. I stood to one side. Art came to greet me, but I felt out of place. I was not sure I had been invited to this banquet, and I feared that I would be turned away without any food. My clothes were inappropriate. I was not dressed like Art, nor like the others. I still wore my Army clothes, in sharp contrast to Art's more formal black tie; and although Art welcomed me in this dream, I felt like a beggar.

While he never told us what to do, Art's understanding of Reality was sufficiently astute to know where the source of authority lay; and I pictured him in my dream as enormously rich, when everyone else, including me, was desperately poor.

In the early days of the trip, when my admiration for Art was untrammelled by any awareness of reality, I had absorbed his words of wisdom as if he had been Moses bringing down the Ten Commandments; and so to have Art appear in my dreams as a sergeant or a banker is not altogether surprising, nor that in my next dream Art appeared dressed like a Cardinal in the Roman Catholic Church. During the first month of the trip, Art always appeared in my dreams dressed in the outer trappings of power.

One evening, early in the trip, while Art had been cooking dinner, the pot had boiled over, and some of our precious food had fallen into the fire. "When the pot boils over, it cools the fire," Art had mused. "In civilization, it just messes up the stove."

At the time, I had thought this comment to be extraordinarily perceptive. How glorious it was to be out in nature where, as he had just pointed out, all things are taken care of in peace and in harmony. How wise Art had seemed! How beautiful Nature seemed. I had engraved those words of wisdom in my heart. Art was not just a sergeant, not just a banker, he was a spiritual authority of very great eminence, like a Cardinal in the Roman Catholic Church: except that his message was different.

On another occasion earlier in the trip, as we worked our way slowly up the rapids and lakes to the height of land, we had stopped for lunch on a beautiful spit of land. It was a lovely day. Art had passed out our ration of three hard-tack biscuits, one with cheese, one with peanut butter, and one with jam.

"Gold!" Joe exclaimed.

I stopped munching my biscuit and looked at Joe.

"Look, Art! Gold!"

Art continued to chew his biscuit. "Probably fool's gold," he said.

Joe scooped some sand from the beach, pinched a golden speck, took out his hunting knife and cut into it. He carried his sample over to Art. "It's not fool's gold, Art. It's the real stuff." Joe thrust the gold under Art's nose. "Look! See! Gold!"

Gold had been discovered on Lake Athabaska, not far from where we had embarked at Stony Rapids. A boom town called "Goldfields" had sprouted up and, next to it, another called "Uranium City." We were travelling over rich ore deposits of uranium and gold.

Art crunched his biscuit. "What this place needs, to improve the scenery, is a gold mine," he said. We all laughed except Joe. Joe returned to where he had been eating and continued to munch his lunch. Before

Art had spoken, we had all taken an interest in Joe's discovery. Now we joked about it.

In those early days of the trip, I had interpreted Art's lack of interest in gold as further proof of his enlightened status. I wanted to enter his spiritual Garden of Eden. A few days before this conversation, I had taken the coins out of my pocket and had thrown them into the lake with great pleasure. It was good to know we had no more use for money in this paradise into which he would be leading us.

My father had been the Senior Partner in a Wall Street banking firm. So had been my grandfather, and my great, great-uncle (L.P. Morton), who had also been Vice-President of the United States under President Harrison. The *Universal Almanac* describes their campaign as one of the most corrupt in U.S. history. My grandmother's summer cottage in Southampton, Long Island had contained five bedrooms for the servants and much larger ones for her guests. The groom and his family lived over the stables a quarter of a mile away, down a beautiful lawn where the odor from the stalls did not mingle with the scent of afternoon tea on the veranda. I had been sent to the "best" schools, Groton and Harvard, as had my father before me; but the money and the corruption had not made anyone happy. My great, great-uncle, the one who had become Vice-President of the United States, had died of syphilis: or at least that was the story I had been told by my mother. My grandfather died of a perforated ulcer when my father was only four. My father committed suicide when I was nineteen. Money had not bought any of them happiness.

At Groton I had rebelled. I had become a Marxist, and I had refused to kneel down in chapel. I had been thrown out of Harvard after only four months. I did not want to follow in the footsteps of my ancestors. I had gone down to the corner of Wall Street and Broad and made speeches denouncing Capitalism, but my father's suicide had taken the edge off my rebellion. Whenever he had been in a room, I had felt at peace, as if everything was being taken care of. Although I adored my father and he had always been kind to me, I did not want to become an investment banker like him. I wanted to escape.

For a while, I had kept company with the wild animals in the back woods of New Hampshire, where my mother owned a summer place, until my mother persuaded Lewis and Virginia Teague to rescue me. I had fallen in love with Virginia, and then escaped into the Army. I tried to be a good soldier, but got court martialled for disrespect to my commanding officer. After my discharge, I escaped to the Arctic with Art.

At first, I felt so happy to be with a man who at last valued something more than money. I had worshipped him and would have been happy to be his disciple, but he preferred his solitude. While I respected his privacy, I had collected his words of wisdom and engraved them in my heart; but now he stood before me in my dreams dressed as a Cardinal in the Roman Catholic Church, this banker of our food supply, this spiritual guru of a religion then alien to me.

In my third dream, Art was standing on a stage in the wilderness, as if on a television show. I felt towards him, now dressed in his scarlet Cardinal's robes, as if he were a great spiritual authority, but a spiritual authority that was slightly out of place in that bleak wilderness of rocks, moss and hunger — to say nothing of the fact that I had, after all, been brought up a Protestant before converting to Marxism, neither tradition friendly to Cardinals in the Roman Catholic hierarchy.

As the trip wore on, I and the others began to question Art's authority. In daily life, Art wore neither the uniform of a sergeant, nor the formal evening dress of a wealthy host, nor the scarlet robes of a Cardinal in the Roman Catholic Church; rather, he wore a frayed work shirt occasionally tucked into blue jeans (more frequently hanging out), an old tennis sweater with holes at the elbows, and, on cold nights, his old Moosehide jacket, along with a well-worn pair of L.L.Bean boots. This was his "uniform," or at least the clothes he wore every day, because he did not have any others: hardly the trappings of an elegant banker or of an army sergeant or of a priest. The only thing that set Art apart from the rest of us (aside from his wisdom, his experience, the wrinkles on his face and the extra large dishes he ate from) was his control of the food.

"Did philosophy die for you?" Saint Paul had asked.

As the days passed into weeks, I forgot about trying to impress Art with my youthful philosophy and thought more about a duck, which I hoped would die for me.

The sun obscured by smoke. Peter Franck and George Grinnell in the red canoe.

Chapter Four
The First Sugar Dispute

One day, as our hunger increased, I reached for my .22 calibre rifle and took aim at a duck. The expedition's artillery was all in the bows of the canoes. The sternmen carried no rifles. Art Moffatt, being a pacifist, had never carried a gun, neither here nor in the War; and Skip and Pete, who had been on other expeditions before with him, Skip twice and Pete once, followed his example. But we novices in the bows were heavily armed, Bruce with a .30-06, Joe with a .30-30, and me with a 22.

"Don't shoot! Don't shoot! It's a mother!" Art yelled.

Reluctantly, I lowered my rifle.

The next day, I made sure the duck was a male and had once again taken aim, but the response from the stern of the grey canoe was the same: "Don't shoot! Don't shoot! It's a mother!"

I lowered my rifle.

We bowmen made a joke of the "Moffatt Maternity League," dedicated to the defense of all mothers, young and old, male and female, and I did not take aim at any more ducks; but as the reality of hunger came more and more to my consciousness, I began to wonder about the wisdom of canoeing through the wilderness under a leader who had just revealed himself as an animal-rights activist.

Sometime in his early childhood, after his mother had died, Art developed the habit of picking up dead birds in the forest and bringing them home to paint them. This horrified his father's housekeeper, so Art then sneaked them up to his bedroom. Possibly he believed that his mother had flown off to heaven as a bird. At any rate, he loved birds and could not bring himself to kill one, starving or not. As I followed Art around, the hunger of my body began to pull me in one direction, the hunger of my soul in the other — caught, as I was, between two realities.

A few days later, a forest fire was burning somewhere close by, and the air was so filled with smoke that we could only see a few feet in front of us. Suddenly trees loomed overhead and our canoes ran up on some rocks. Art decided we might as well make camp, but we did not know whether we were on an island or on the mainland. We also did not know how far away the fire was or whether it was coming our way. We were nervous that night. When a house catches fire and fills with smoke, one escapes outdoors; but we had already escaped outdoors. I felt trapped. There was no refuge for us in this endless wilderness which was now suffocating us in smoke.

Because we had landed early, Skip took the opportunity to check our supplies. After dinner, he announced that if we continued consuming sugar at the current rate, we would run out before the trip was half over. He asked what we thought we should do about it, and then scowled disapprovingly as if we had been guilty of being hungry.

As the smoke thickened, my anxiety increased. I felt short of breath. I wondered if I were really suffocating, or just scared to death.

"Divide up the sugar six ways," Joe demanded and scowled back at Skip. "Let everyone look after his own!"

All our food was rationed except tea, milk and sugar. Art was fond of tea and had brought plenty, but not plenty of sugar to sweeten it with.

Art sat on a rock and sipped his tea from a China cup. His wife had given him this sacred cup, and he had carried it on all his trips. Every morning after breakfast, and every evening after dinner, he would sit for hours holding the China cup in both hands absorbing the warmth of it. It was his most sentimental possession, and over the years he had held it so often that the rose painted on the side was nearly worn off. We were all sipping our tea that evening, but the rest of us held standard plastic mugs that were ugly and had no sentimental value.

Every morning at breakfast, and every evening at dinner, sugar in an open press-top tin had been placed on a rock near the campfire where we were allowed to help ourselves. Art had rationed neither the sugar, nor the milk, nor the tea into which we heaped the sugar; and, because everything else was rationed, the heaps of sugar had grown higher and higher, and the cups of tea we drank more and more numerous.

Peter Franck, Bruce, and I supported Joe's suggestion of dividing up the remaining sugar six ways so that we could ration our own.

Bruce LeFavour, Skip's bowman, asked Skip what he thought should be done. Skip stood on the higher ground, and refused to express his "interests, appetites or passions," as if he did not have any. He just scowled disapprovingly at the rest of us because we did, and then he topped off his disapproval with a lecture on "group consideration and altruistic behavior" like a 19th Century moralist.

I thought Joe's suggestion of dividing up the sugar six ways would carry for lack of any alternative, but finally Art intervened and vetoed the idea.

"There's no need," he said. "Just restrict yourselves to two spoonfuls for a bowl of oatmeal and one spoonful for a cup of tea. Be on your honor not to take too much."

Art's gracious "honor system" was carried unanimously because he had suggested it; but after a while, Joe began to chuckle. When asked what was funny, he talked about the image of us trying to curb our hunger by an "honor system."

The obvious way around Art's "honor system" had occurred to Joe, as it had occurred to me: and I began to laugh at Joe's description of us wetting our spoons before scooping them into the sugar bucket so as to make the grains of sugar stick to their underside as well as to their tops, or "accidentally" spilling a little tea in the sugar bucket to make lumps.

I was soon rolling on the ground in uncontrollable laughter as Joe spat on his spoon to show how much more sugar would stick to it under the new "honor system."

I was faced with a choice of two realities, the noble reality of Skip, or the hungry reality of Joe. Skip was admirable, but Joe was realistic. Before we left civilization, I had wanted to transform myself into a more noble human being like Skip: but now I could not stop laughing.

A secondary effect of Art's "honor system" was the need to pee during the night. Art had restricted the amount of sugar we placed in each cup of tea, but not the number of cups of tea we could drink. Joe created an imaginary scene with everyone pretending not to notice how many times we were all accidentally meeting in the middle of the night to "look at the stars."

The more Joe elaborated, the more I laughed, until I was in near hysterics, choking on the smoke and holding my belly in pain.

Art smiled.

Skip scowled.

Pete looked puzzled.

Bruce looked back and forth, sometimes scowling, sometimes laughing, depending on whom he made eye contact with: Joe, his former roommate at Dartmouth, or Skip, the high-principled second-in-command. When Skip looked back at Bruce, Bruce stopped laughing and scowled also.

On Selwyn Lake as we approached the height of land, I suggested to my sternman, Peter Franck, that we change the sides we had been paddling on for the previous three weeks. "If we don't change, we'll become lopsided," I argued.

"Art's not l-l-lopsided," Peter said.

We both looked over at Art: his left shoulder was hanging lower than his right.

"Art n-n-never changes," Peter said and continued to paddle on the same side, just as he and Art had done since the beginning of the trip.

photo credit George Luste

Losing the trees

Chapter Five
Panic

After climbing up the rapids of the Chipman River for nearly a month, we approached the Height of Land. It was a low range of hills. Behind us, the rivers flowed south, back towards civilization; ahead, they flowed north towards the Arctic Ocean, although some were diverted east into Hudson Bay when they ran into the Thelon River.

Art called for a holiday. Two weeks had passed since our last one, so it was not an unreasonable request; but idleness gave me time to think, and the more I thought, the more scared I became. By dinner time, I was in an advanced state of terror.

I convinced myself that I was going to break a leg. I would get appendicitis. We would run out of food and I would starve to death. We would capsize in a rapids and I would drown. I would surely freeze to death if nothing else killed me first. I became absolutely certain I was going to die. My desire to follow Art into the wilderness was diminishing with each passing thought until, by dinner time, I was ready to pack up and go home. The expedition seemed to me to be madness.

It would be easy to return home now. All we had to do was turn around; but once over the Height of Land, the rivers flowed in the wrong direction, away from civilization, not towards it. We would be trapped by the rapids. We would be forced to continue down the river to an inevitable death. I wanted to paddle back to civilization and safety.

We were losing the trees, another broken link with civilization, which also made me nervous. Trees provided wood for our fires. On the Barrens there would be no trees. No protection from the cold Arctic blizzards. If we lost our paddles in a rapids, we could not fashion new ones from the trees, because there would be no trees. If our tent poles broke, we would be unable to replace them. Across the Height of Land, I imagined Arctic bleakness and frozen death. That evening at dinner, I was silent. I did not want the others to know how frightened I was.

Dinners were usually happy, noisy affairs, with much laughter and kidding around; but that evening everyone was silent. Finally, while we were sipping our tea, Bruce LeFavour, the great conversationalist, said: "Say, Art, you know that story about Hornby and Christian, what really happened, anyway?"

Suddenly we all began talking, pressing Art for more details. Art sipped his tea and did not volunteer much information. Finally, he got up and left the campfire.

John Hornby had been an adventurer like Art. Before the First World War, he had fled into the wilderness. First, he went alone; then, after the War,

42

with Captain Bullock; and then a third time with two young men, Harold Adlard, twenty-seven, and Edgar Christian (Hornby's nephew), who had just turned eighteen.

"You are out to lay the foundations of your life," Edgar's father had written, "and all your future depends on how you face the next few years."

Hornby, Adlard and Christian had built a cabin on the Thelon River, a river we would join before the end of the trip; but the caribou had not arrived that Autumn in the region, and all three men had starved. Hornby died in April, Adlard in May, and Christian in June, four days shy of his birthday. He left a final note for his mother.

Dear Mother,

Feeling weak now can only write a little. Sorry left it so late but alas I have struggled hard. Please don't blame dear Jack. He loved you and me only in this world and tell no one else this but keep it and believe.

Ever loving & thankful to you for all a dear mother is to a boy & has been to me.

Bye Bye Love to all.

Christian's father had supported the trip, believing it would build his son's "character;" but the character of a cannibal was not, perhaps, what his father had in mind. The caribou returned before Christian died; but either he was too weak to shoot one, or he had lost the desire. In his diary, Christian noted that he had "plenty of meat to eat" near the end; but it was on the lean side, and apparently not of the kind that laid the foundations of the British Empire. Edgar Christian put his diary in the stove and pulled a Hudson's Bay blanket over his head.

The bodies were discovered a year later by four young prospectors paddling down the Thelon. The RCMP, represented by an Inspector Trundle, managed to reach the site on the 25th of July, 1929, two years after Christian, Adlard and Hornby had died. Trundle reported possible evidence of cannibalism.

That evening we imagined ourselves writing similar notes:

Dear Mother,
Please don't blame dear Art....

However, noble sentiments aside, I was terrified.

The Mountie stared at me, as if waiting for an answer.

"... so you lost your sense of reality."

I stared back.

photo credit Sports Illustrated

Carol and Arthur Moffatt

Chapter Six
The Broken Tea Cup

The reality of my dreams created a very different image of Art than the one recorded in his diary. On the Height of Land, I had dreamed of him dressed in the robes of a Cardinal in the Roman Catholic Church; but that evening, the concerns he expressed in his diary were more mundane.

July 21st, Anniversary day: Carol and I have been married 10 years. Ten years, two daughters, a house, and here I am, in the biggest wilderness in North America.

And this morning, as I loaded the canoe, I felt pretty certain that what I have been suspecting for three or four days is true — namely, that I've started a small hernia in my left groin. It is not particularly painful — there is a small lump about as big as the end of my thumb there; but after lifting the packs and camera boxes, the groin is tired and sore. Then as I paddle, the sensation is with me all day, though much of the time it feels perfectly normal.

This brings up a big question. Whether to continue the trip. Going back would be relatively easy, except for the long portages, and safe. Going on is an unknown quantity — though I can be sure it won't be easy — and there isn't much chance I'll be able to get back, once we start down the river. We are only about one-quarter of the way to Baker Lake, if that far.

If I go on, the hernia, if it is really one, will probably get worse. Can I depend on the men to help me? Not very well — it takes two men to paddle each canoe, and load and unload. Further, the men would not want to — or be able to — help when tired. Still, the thing might not get worse. If it doesn't everything will be all right.

The next day, we completed the portage across the Height of Land. The box which contained our dishes came open and Art's sacred China tea cup with the worn rose fell on a rock and broke.

When Art came down the portage and saw his cup in pieces, he sat on a rock and did not speak. Two hours later, he was still sitting on the rock and still not speaking.

Not just the date (his Tenth Wedding Anniversary), but the place, the headwaters of the Dubawnt River, were inauspicious. The Dubawnt flows from the Height of Land north into the Arctic for about five hundred miles before joining the Thelon and turning east towards Hudson Bay. No one lives on the shores of the Dubawnt, which is why Art had come to photograph it. It is the last Garden of Eden.

In the Autumn, the Chipewyans leave Stony Rapids and climb up the Chipman River to the Height of Land to hunt and trap. They cross the Height of Land, but do not venture far down the Dubawnt because of the difficulty of portaging back up it. In winter, the caribou take shelter in the southern forests, and so do the Chipewyans.

In the Summer, the caribou migrate north to the Arctic Circle, and the Innuit come in from the shores of the Arctic Ocean and Hudson Bay to hunt them. They work their way up the Thelon and Dubawnt Rivers to Dubawnt Lake, but not much beyond. Traditionally, the Chipewyans and the Innuit have killed one another on contact, so they tend to leave a large stretch of "no man's land" between them. Every imaginable migratory bird nests there. The lakes are teaming with fish. The wolves follow the migrating caribou herds picking off stragglers, and the musk ox gather in circles to defend themselves; but few people have ever disturbed the peace of this all too natural world

Before coming on the trip, Art had been faced with three choices. He needed money to feed his family. He could either go down to New York and do as others in Western Civilization were doing, ("pave over paradise with a parking lot"); or he could double his life insurance policy and buy a one-way ticket to the Great Beyond; or he could gamble on a wildlife film. He chose the last two.

Of the three alternatives, he preferred to gamble on the wildlife film; but movies do not bring to their viewers the gentleness, the inner peace, and the sense of being "lucky" that Art had discovered in the wilderness. What the movie would do for Art was to buy him time; but with the broken tea cup at his feet, he could not repress his sense of foreboding.

The movie was not working out. To be a good wildlife photographer, one has to sit and wait like a hunter; and we did not have time to sit and wait. If we waited, we would be caught in the autumn freeze-up.

Art had been able to take some footage of an Arctic tern trying to poke out Bruce LeFavour's eyes when the green canoe chanced too close to an island where the bird had nested, but Art had not captured on film anything that would pay enough to feed his family when the expedition was over.

With his broken tea cup lying shattered at his feet, Art became convinced that he would never see his wife and children again, and so he sat, and so we waited.

A forest fire was burning near by. Finally Skip intruded on Art's meditation and suggested that the fire would provide some good pictures. Art picked up his camera, and paddled over to it.

There had always been forest fires burning around us. Some days, as many as five; but this was to be the last fire we would see, because it was also the last forest. The forests had become more open, as in parks. The ground was covered with dry, pale green "caribou moss," a kind of lichen which crunches under foot when stepped on. The fire moved along the lichen till it came to a tree; the flames climbed the bark. Suddenly an explosion of steam billowed forth as the sap boiled off. Immediately after the steam, the tree burst into flames.

There was little danger for us because the trees were small and far apart. We were able to walk back and forth through the line of fire as it moved towards the lake. Art seemed happy with the pictures; and the following day, across the Continental Divide, we continued on our way while the fragments of his cherished China tea cup lay shattered on a rock.

My fellow bowmen
Joe Lanouette above & Bruce LeFavour below.

Chapter Seven
The United Bowmen's Association

In the beginning of the trip, there was one leader. After about a month, there were six leaders, all heading in different directions.

We three bowmen had never been on a long-distance canoe trip; so, at first, we were eager to learn from Art. But after a month of paddling, I felt I knew all there was to know and could lead the expedition at least as well as he — and the other two bowmen seemed to have come to parallel conclusions. After crossing the Height of Land, we formed a union and went into revolt.

At first, the most mysterious part of the expedition had been the provisioning. How had Art planned, packed, and preserved enough food to get us across the largest uninhabited area in North America where the unexpected would be a way of life?

Before the trip had begun, we were only too grateful to Art for his wisdom and his experience; but by the time we had worked our way up the river to the Height of Land, we bowmen felt we had lifted this mysterious veil and could have done a better job.

Art's provisioning technique had been amazingly simple. On his previous trips, he had discovered how much oatmeal was eaten each day: about three times as much as one would have believed possible. He had multiplied this figure by eighty, added a little extra for emergencies, and then purchased at the Hudson's Bay Post one hundred bags of oatmeal. So much for the mystique of planning breakfast.

Planning lunch had been almost as simple. In northern Hudson's Bay stores, they sell "hard tack" or "pilot" biscuits. These are slow baked, plain, white flour biscuits equivalent to three or four pieces of stale white bread from which all the moisture (and probably the nourishment) has been removed. Because they are dry, they do not go mouldy. Art had discovered that if one washed three of these biscuits down with enough water, the biscuits would swell up in one's belly and make one feel full. To top off the full-stomach feeling with a touch of substance, he coated each biscuit with peanut butter, jam or cheese.

We were getting plenty of exercise, so vitamins were not as important to us as calories. These coated hard tack biscuits had lots of calories: eating them was one of the three high points of the day — along with breakfast and supper. As with planning the day's first meal, the arithmetic was simple: three hard tack biscuits per man, times six, times eighty worked out to be about a hundred boxes of biscuits.

Likewise with the cheese, peanut butter and jam. He divided one package of Velveeta processed cheese six ways each day, times eighty days, yielding a case of cheeses. A small can of jam or a jar of peanut butter lasted about two or three days, so we carried a couple of cases of jam and peanut butter.

The arithmetic for dinner was the same as that for lunch and breakfast. The secret to Art's amazing success as a provider was his skill at choosing the cheapest items in the Hudson's Bay store and then buying not quite enough of them. Before starting the trip, we had handed over to him $200 apiece for our three months supply of food, or about two dollars a day per man, which we felt was reasonable enough until we had spent forty days hungry in the wilderness: and then we went into revolt.

For dinner, it was the same simple arithmetic: two boxes of macaroni, two cans of tomato paste, two cans of "Spork" or "Spam," and two packages of dehydrated soup, times eighty. Everything was simple, provided we all ate the same food every day, and provided we reached the Hudson's Bay Post at Baker Lake before the food ran out. But Bruce LeFavour, who liked to cook, had become miffed at Art for his lack of interest in culinary artistry; and we other two bowmen equally so because, as the trip progressed, we became increasingly aware that we did not have nearly enough food to reach our destination.

It seemed to us that Art's only recipe for a good meal was to make sure we all came to dinner hungry. When hungry, everything tastes good, even mouldy oatmeal; so why go through the expense of buying costly foods?

As for the other aspects of planning the trip, we bowmen felt that we had unveiled the mystery of these as well. Travelling seven or eight hundred miles across the Barrens may sound exciting, especially when there are great splotches of white on the maps with the word "unmapped" stamped on them; but as activities go, paddling and portaging can be as boring as any other daily routine. One spends the day paddling towards that distant horizon where sky and water meet; and by the time one reaches that horizon, the next horizon looks very much the same.

Canoes travel about two miles an hour, or about ten miles in a five-hour day. Some days are too windy to paddle, of course, but it is perfectly possible to paddle twenty, thirty, even forty miles on a calm day; and so we had become puzzled by our slow rate of travel. In fact, we had the sensation of getting absolutely nowhere.

In the beginning of the trip, our slowness could be excused by our heavy loads and the long portages. We averaged only one mile a day on portages because we had to make four or five trips; that is to say, we had to walk seven or nine miles back and forth for every mile forward — and our loads were heavy, between sixty and a hundred pounds per trip. Later, we were to discover that our slowness was owing to other causes. Ten miles a day would have been a reasonable average for a trip from Hudson's Bay Post to Hudson's Bay Post across the Barrens, but not for a spiritual voyage into the Garden of Eden, or wherever it was that Art was taking us.

Two days after we had crossed the Height of Land, Art called the noon break for lunch. We bowmen threw an arm or leg over each other's gunwales to keep the canoes from drifting apart, and the sternmen did the same, while Art scrounged around in the luncheon pack for the biscuits. He passed them up to us bowmen on the blade of his paddle. While we were munching our biscuits, and the sternmen were munching theirs, the eighteen-foot length of the canoes separated us. We bowmen could not hear what the sternmen were talking about, and they could not hear us. So we were free to slander each other with impunity, except that from their point of view, we were not worth gossiping about.

"Say, Joe, what are your thoughts about Art's schedule?" Bruce asked. Bruce was always kind enough, or insecure enough, to ask our opinions before expressing one of his own.

Joe exploded: "What schedule! Art takes off for one of his 'spiritual' bird walks, and leaves me to strike our tent and pack up, and I never know when he will be ready to shove off!"

Bruce nodded his head encouragingly for every one of Joe's complaints until Joe was all complained out, his dark eyes flashing angrily under black hair; and then Bruce turned to me and asked what I thought.

I agreed with Joe. In the beginning of the trip, I had thought that I would have been willing to put aside my own "interests, appetites and passions,"as a spiritual sacrifice on the altar of the "higher good;" but after nearly forty days in the wilderness on short rations, I was bored. My panic of a few days earlier had mostly faded away, but I wanted a more definite schedule. I wanted the assurance that we would eventually reach the Hudson's Bay Post at Baker Lake on September 2nd, as planned, and a schedule seemed to me the best way of guaranteeing that. Also a schedule would make the trip more enjoyable. I would know when and if I could be free to read a book or explore the back country away from the river.

My fellow bowmen seemed to feel much the same way, because Bruce soon progressed a step by asking Joe if he thought we bowmen had enough say in how the expedition was run.

Joe had high cheekbones and an angular nose. He came from Brazil; and after the trip, when he had become an editor of the *National Geographic*, he was known as "Indian Joe." The more Joe's nostrils flared, the more vigorously Bruce nodded.

It seemed to us bowmen that the expedition lacked structure. Art and Skip would discuss the weather, discuss the food supply, discuss our progress, discuss Art's movie; but we bowmen were never consulted. Everything seemed to be based on the whimsy of the sternmen.

Peter Franck sat back with the sternmen silently. He was included in their conversations because he sat with them in the stern, but he rarely said anything. Up in the bow, we felt totally ignored. By the end of lunch, we bowmen had formed the "United Bowmen's Association" and had agreed to go on strike if Art and the two other sternmen did not comply with our demands.

Bruce turned to me and suggested that I be the spokesman for the Association because I was the eldest of the bowmen and because, as Bruce put it, "Art likes you."

Bruce and Joe had been roommates at Dartmouth, and the sternmen had all known each other before coming on the trip. Skip had been down the Albany twice with Art, and Pete once. I was the only one who was a complete outsider.

I was grateful that Bruce and Joe made a point of including me in their conversations, and I was flattered that they appointed me to be their spokesman in our newly-formed Association. But once again I found myself in the role of rebel.

Before my father's death, I had spent my young life like an Islamic fundamentalist, walking around town looking for a school bus to blow up in the name of God (figuratively speaking). I had done my best to blow up Groton, to blow up Harvard, to blow up the United States Army; and here I was elected to blow up Art. Every time I had rebelled, I had succeeded only in hurting those persons who were trying to love me: me, this self-righteous angel of destruction.

At Groton, I had received a record number of "Black Marks." The Headmaster had recommended to my parents that I be sent to summer school, not to improve my grades, but to curb my rebellion. When that did not work, the school had suggested a psychiatrist.

At Harvard, I had managed to get myself turfed out by denouncing the capitalist system on all my midterm exams. Perhaps it had been just coincidence, but my father had committed suicide shortly thereafter.

In the Army, I had been court-martialled for disrespect to my commanding officer. Self-righteous as always, I was defending six friends of mine who had been accused of something they had not done. My Captain let them go, and court-martialled me for disrespect instead.

There are three kinds of courts-martial in the Army: Summary, Special and General. In the Summary, the judge is also the prosecutor. "Bring the guilty bastard in," is the traditional way of opening these proceedings. I was found guilty, busted from Corporal to Private, and sentenced to three months in the Stockade. Although my rank was reduced, I did not have to serve time in the Stockade, because my unit was ordered out on maneuvers and my skills as a Signals Corps technician were required for the exercise.

The Inspector General explained to me that, in the Army, justice is for the benefit of the Army — not for the benefit of the individual. He asked if I wanted to be transferred out of my outfit.

I said no.

Four months later, when my two-year tour of duty was up, I was called into a room along with the other "short timers." Our Captain, the same man who had court-martialled me, gave us all a pep-talk about re-enlistment. When he had court-martialled me, the Captain had been new to my outfit. He had learned later that I had been a good soldier, one of the few who would volunteer for extra duties. Now as I was about to be discharged, he turned to me. "The Army has need of good soldiers," he said.

This Captain was a black man who had won an athletic scholarship to college. Everywhere but in the Army, he had been greeted with prejudice. He loved the army, and now he turned to me and invited me to join him. He had actually been a good officer; and, despite our initial run-in, I had come to respect him. Nevertheless, I shook my head.

"What will you do on the outside?"

"Shine shoes, I guess."

My black Captain looked at me.

One hundred and twenty-six of my ancestors had been officers in the American Army during the War of Independence. Earlier, during the French and Indian Wars, one of my ancestors was Major General Preble, who had out-ranked George Washington when they both served in the colonial forces; and well over a century later, still another had been the Commanding Officer at West Point while my black Captain's ancestors were presumably shining shoes.

My Captain looked at his shoes. Prejudice had caught up with him even in his beloved Army.

There is a joke about a husband who found the Bishop in bed with his wife. He went to the window and began blessing the people on the street.

"What on Earth are you doing!" the Bishop exclaimed.

"Since you have taken over my duties, I thought I would take over yours," the husband replied: and I suppose, deep in my soul, I felt that I should be the commanding officer and my Captain the polisher of boots. But unlike the Bishop, my Captain had performed his duties faithfully; and unlike the injured husband, I had not been betrayed — and it was the curse of prejudice I was dispensing. I was not fit to shine my Captain's shoes.

I turned in my seat and announced to Art that we bowmen, "the underprivileged working class" as I tried to represent us, would go on strike if we were not given a schedule.

There was great jeering and laughter from the sternmen at the idea that we bowmen knew the meaning of the word "work." After the commotion died down, Art mumbled something to the effect that "the wind does not blow on schedule, nor the rain fall on schedule."

That was the whole point! We bowmen were tired of being governed by the anarchy of wind and rain, as interpreted by a mystical guru whose only desire seemed to be to surrender to forces more powerful than he. We wanted to be "masters of our fate and captains of our destinies," as the poet Walt Whitman had phrased it. We wanted to conquer nature, not surrender to it!

After a while, Art picked up his paddle and continued down the lake. Skip and Pete, the other two sternmen, followed Art's lead as they always had done; but this time, we bowmen did not imitate the guru. Instead, we leaned back on the packs and held our paddles in the air "on strike."

In *The Brothers Karamazov,* Dostoevsky has Jesus kiss the Grand Inquisitor on the cheek. I wanted Art to play the role of the Grand Inquisitor. Like Dostoevsky, I had been a rebel, but now my rebellion was of a different nature: it was not so much against authority, as against Art's refusal to be an authority. Who would have thought that I, the rebel, would have actually wished for the hierarchies of civilization to protect me from this wilderness anarchy? That I, this atheist, Marxist, pacifist, would have preferred Art to take on the role of an Army sergeant, or of a wealthy banker who could afford to feed us, or of a Cardinal in the Roman Catholic Church, or even of the Grand Inquisitor, that I would have wanted Art to become an archetype of some male-dominated hierarchical structure, any hierarchical structure, if only it would carry me back to civilization where I could once again fill my belly full to overflowing and have the luxury of rebelling against all those evil structures of civilization in warmth, comfort and safety?

As I had become more afraid, I had developed more and more doubts about Art's spiritual status. Standing on the stage in the wilderness, dressed in a Cardinal's scarlet robes, all his spiritual wisdom had seemed no match for the endless land beyond, the "miles and miles of nothing but miles and miles."

"... we, the underprivileged working class...."

The shadow of doubt had fallen across the stage of my dreams on which Art had been standing with such an ambience of power; but if I had dreamed of Art as an authority, and then rebelled against his lack of authority, Art had other concerns. He did not reply to my demands, he simply continued to paddle down the lake.

After a while Bruce, not wishing to antagonize Skip, sat up and began to paddle — and then Joe and I also. The "strike" was broken.

Two days later, a storm came up. We were held prisoner on a spit of land for the next four days. At midnight of the fourth day, Art began packing his canoe; the wind had finally died enough for us to continue our journey. Waves broke on the rocks as we picked our way cautiously through the early morning darkness.

Around three A.M. the rising sun burned the mackerel skies a brilliant crimson, and we felt current sucking the canoes out of the lake into the fast Dubawnt River. Art pulled the grey canoe into an eddy, and disembarked on shore. He built a fire and brewed a pot of hot chocolate which we sipped while overlooking the Dubawnt under the golden sun of dawn.

At those latitudes in Summer, the sun had swung around the northern horizon glowing pink all night long, and then burned the bottom off the clouds in sparkling tones of fire. We sipped our hot chocolate, warmed ourselves in the morning sun, basked in the beauty of the natural world, and forgot for the time being our demand for a nine-to-five schedule.

The red canoe
Peter Franck above & George Grinnell below.

The author seven years
prior to trip.

The author today.

photo credit Sports Illustrated

66

Chapter Eight
Separate Ways

Our Chestnut canoes were wonderful. Too bad the company went out of business. The many layers of canvas seemed to be more than a quarter inch thick, and the ribs were close together and strong. They cracked, but none of the canoes broke in two or fell apart.

Before we got to the bottom of our first rapids, Peter Franck and I had smashed into yet another boulder. This was Pete's first rapids as a sternman; and, when we were done, Art asked Pete if he wanted to shoot any more. Pete never uttered a word of complaint about me or my uncontrollable technique; he just nodded his head.

The morning after my day of panic, just two days before the shattering of Art's sacred cup, I had been reading Gibbon's *The Decline and Fall of the Roman Empire* when the tent Pete and I were sharing collapsed on me. I poked my head out the entrance and saw Pete pulling out the tent pegs. I pointed out to him that Art was still sitting by the fire sipping his breakfast tea and showing no signs of packing up or getting ready to leave, but Peter went about his business without replying. Soon, he had launched, loaded, and boarded our red canoe; we sat in it for two hours waiting for Art.

I suggested that we might as well push off and head up the lake. Peter said nothing, but retained his hold on one of the shore rocks.

Peter and Art had liked each other when they had descended the Albany River a few years before. They were both slightly built, and both strong and determined in a quiet, introspective way. Because of their mutual respect, Art had invited Peter to join him on this trip; but Peter, like us bowmen, was beginning to go in a different direction.

On Art's previous Albany trips, things had been run on schedule. Art had been down the Albany six times and knew what lay around every bend. There were three Cree villages along that river where he was able to replenish supplies; and he had always arrived at the end of the trip in time to catch the boat from Fort Albany to Moosenee that carried him and his charges back to the railhead and civilization on schedule.

Pete had been seventeen at the time he had joined Art on that earlier venture. His parents had paid Art for the trip; and it had been Art's job to see that Pete, Skip and their other young companions were returned home safely and on time, which Art had done. But he had organized our Dubawnt trip with a very different purpose in mind. He was not being paid by parents to look after us, and so his attention was focused on other things more dear to his heart. But what was dear to Art's heart was not always dear to Peter's heart.

Pete expressed his desires through actions. He was the first across the portages, the first to get ready in the mornings, and the first to launch his canoe; but Art did not seem to get the message. In his diary, Art had only noted that Pete and I were, as he put it, "iron men." We never rested on the portages, and our canoe tended to inch ahead of the others on the lakes if we did not hold ourselves in check.

As time passed, Peter Franck, like us bowmen, had become increasingly worried that we would run out of food before we would reach the outpost at Baker Lake. About once a week, his rear end could be seen sticking out from under an overturned canoe while he made an inventory of our remaining supplies. By the end of the third week, he had begun to save empty jam tins and peanut butter jars into which he placed bits of his lunch ration, in preparation for the inevitable day when our food ran out.

Joe had noticed Peter saving pieces of his hard tack biscuit one day and had teased him. "If we ran out of food and were starving, surely you would share your cache with us," Joe said. Joe himself had been teased earlier in the trip when we discovered that he had brought with him a private supply of chocolate bars and gourmet cheeses in his extra-large personal pack.

When Pete did not reply, Bruce LeFavour repeated the question.

"S-s-save y-y-your own," Pete stammered. He always seemed reluctant to speak, perhaps because he had a tendency to stammer.

Although Pete and I shared a canoe and a tent, the number of sentences we spoke to one another could have been counted on one hand. One evening early in the trip, my air mattress slid over onto his half of our "A-frame" mountain tent. He protested, and we dropped an imaginary plumb line down from the center seam to the floor; he made a mark, and the issue never arose again. "Good fences make good neighbors," as the poet Robert Frost noted.

I liked pitching our tent high on a hill where the view was good and the wind kept the bugs away; the others generally pitched their tents as close to the canoes and to the campfire as possible where it was more sociable, and where they did not have to carry their packs as far. Bruce and Joe dubbed Pete and me "the honeymooners," because we kept to ourselves and never seemed to fight. Living with Peter was like living with a Trappist monk, he so rarely spoke.

At first, Peter didn't seem to mind where I pitched the tent, and seemed happy to be aloof from the others; but one evening a frightening thunder storm struck, and a blue ball of lighting rolled through the tent between our two air mattresses. A few days later, I again pitched our tent high on a hill; but when I returned to it after dinner, I discovered that Pete had moved it, and thereafter I frequently found our tent moved to a more secure location.

We did have some minor disputes, but they were non-verbal ones. When we set off in the canoes some mornings, my back would sometimes be a bit stiff. I generally attributed my discomfort to the load in the canoe being unbalanced. To counter this apparent lack of balance, I would slide over in my seat and sit closer to the gunwale, thus tipping the canoe to the side on which I paddled.

Shortly after, I would feel a jerking motion in the stern as Peter slid over in the opposite direction. I would then slide further to the right, and he further to the left, until we were both hanging out of the canoe on different sides. Eventually we would stop paddling and "adjust the load." He would move packs over in one direction, and I in the other. This would go on for the first hour or two in the morning, and then my back would stop hurting; and we would give up shifting around and paddle down the lake, half asleep out of boredom.

Another silent confrontation occurred when we "kicked the poles." Early in the trip, Art had cut fifteen black spruce poles, averaging about twelve feet in length. He used nine of them to build a frame for the kitchen tarpaulin: a total of six for a tripod at each end, another for a ridge pole to throw the tarp over, and a pole on each side at the base to tie the tarp down. We also carried six spares in case any of them broke on the Barrens, where no trees grew above knee-high. The Chipewyans call the Barrens "the land of the little sticks." In the Arctic proper, there are not even little sticks, so we carried our own big sticks.

We were very glad that Art had had the foresight to cut these poles while we were still in the boreal forest because they served a triple purpose. In shallow rapids, we also used some of them to brake the canoes and others to elevate the canoe packs. Our canoes were not covered, so we frequently took in water. On the lakes, waves washed aboard; in the rapids, spray came over the bows; and on rainy days, the drops collected and sloshed around in the bottoms of the canoes. Our canoe packs were made of canvas which repelled the spray and the rain, but they were not waterproof; so by elevating them off the bottom of the canoes on top of these poles, we kept our oatmeal dry, or more or less dry. Sooner or later, of course, everything went mouldy that could go mouldy; but by setting the canoe packs on top of these poles, it went mouldy less rapidly.

Cutting these poles had been a good idea, but they were uncomfortable under foot. They extended the length of the canoe nearly from stem to stern. The canoes, eighteen-foot "prospector" models, didn't easily accommodate the varying lengths of the poles, ranging from twelve to fifteen feet: long enough to reach from my feet in the bow to Peter's feet in the stern. Those sticks may have been useful for keeping the packs out of the bilge water, but they were also uncomfortable to rest our feet on.

At some point during the paddling day, the discomfort of having the poles under foot would get to me, and I would nudge them back towards the stern with the heel of my boot. A half an hour later or so, I would notice that the poles had returned to their original position. For three months, those poles were nudged back and forth between Peter and me, and we never spoke a word.

Our almost total lack of verbal communication had its advantages and its disadvantages. The advantages were that we inhabited our own little worlds whose orbits rarely crossed, except when the poles got underfoot or my air mattress infringed upon his, or I pitched our tent in a location he did not like. The disadvantages, however, became apparent when we tried to shoot that first rapids.

For the first month, we had been travelling upstream to the Height of Land and thus portaging up rapids; but once over the Height of Land, we began shooting downstream. At our first downstream rapids, Art pulled his canoe to the bank and scouted ahead with Skip and Pete, the other two sternmen. Bruce, Joe and I, the three bowmen, were left upstream to hold the canoes.

When the sternmen returned, Art and Joe pushed off in the grey canoe and shot the rapids with no problem. Next, it was our turn; but of course Pete and I never bothered to discuss how we planned to shoot it. I had made certain assumptions, and he had made certain others; and we did not discover our differences until the river rounded a bend.

The others were waiting for us downstream. Joe, in the bow of the grey canoe, laughed. Art, watching us from the stern of the grey canoe, looked concerned.

There are two ways of shooting a rapids. In the old-fashioned way, the bowman provides the power, and the sternman sticks his paddle out the stern to act as a rudder. In the old-fashioned way, the idea is to go through the rapids as fast as possible and to keep the bow pointed downstream at all times.

In the previous century, there were no dams on the major rivers, so the volume of water through rapids was very much heavier than it is on most southern rivers today. In high-volume rapids, the danger of hitting boulders is slight; but the danger of swamping is high. Speed enables the old-fashioned canoeist to crash through the high "standing" waves found at the bottom of chutes, and to avoid being capsized by being turned broadside to the current when the bow hits a back eddy; but today, high-volume rapids are hard to find, unless one happens to be canoeing in the far north — as were we.

In the south, the dangers are from "rock gardens" rather than from big waves. To suit the different conditions, modern canoeists have abandoned the traditional methods. The bowman does the steering, and the sternman eases the canoe down the rapids by back-paddling. Modern recreational canoeists generally travel light; they are apt to be carrying supplies for only a week or two — not a year's supply of beaver pelts or trade goods weighing a ton. Light canoes can be turned quickly in a rapids, and if the canoe is also decked over, the modern recreational canoeist can "play" in the rapids; that is to say, duck into backwaters, quarter the standing waves, "ferry" across the river and weave through shallows.

Art had taught himself how to shoot rapids when alone on the Albany River at seventeen. He had had no bowman to provide power, so he shot the rapids slowly and carefully, working his way down in harmony with the current and the back eddies. In general, Art's philosophy of shooting rapids was a compromise between the old and the new. Art did not believe in slam-banging through anything, least of all down rapids, which were sacred symbols of the natural reconciliation between land and water. If the rapids were too rough, Art simply portaged around them. Peter Franck had learned to shoot rapids from Art.

When Peter and I entered our first rapids without exchanging a word, I assumed we would be crashing down them in the old-fashioned way. I dug my paddle strongly into the river and drove our canoe forward with all my strength. At Groton, I had been captain of the "Crew." In the Army, I had received a bracelet for being the "most physically fit" man in my battalion. I put all my strength into the paddle and the blade bent. We shot down the rapids at full speed.

I could feel Pete's agitated shifting back and forth on his stern seat as the canoe careened this way and that and finally slammed into a boulder on the bank when the river rounded a bend. I heard the stem crack. The current swung the stern around and carried us sideways downstream. We straightened ourselves out in time to run full speed over another boulder. I heard the ribs cracking under my right foot as I drove the canoe over the top with all my strength.

Pete and I survived those first rapids; but of the three crews on the expedition, our technique was considered to be the most laughable.

The day Art died, no one was laughing.

photo credit Joe Lanouette

Bruce LeFavour and Skip Pessl in the green canoe.

Chapter Nine
The Second Sugar Dispute

The following day, we came to a rapids about which Art and Skip disagreed. Skip thought he could shoot it. Art thought it more advisable to portage, but he was willing to let Skip try his skill if he wanted.

The green canoe, with Bruce in the bow and Skip in the stern, descended the chute, crashed through the standing waves, and negotiated the boulders downstream without capsizing. Skip held his paddle in the air triumphantly, and so Pete and I followed him down in our red canoe.

We crashed through everything at full speed and experienced no more difficulty than had Skip and Bruce; but Art and Joe, moving more leisurely in their grey canoe, soon had their gunwales awash and only barely made it to the safety of a shallow back eddy before rolling over. Standing waist deep in water, they threw their packs up on the bank.

Both Art and Skip had been proven right about this rapids. Skip did not mind going strongly into the standing waves at the foot of the chute, but Art was in the habit of going more gently. Skip's judgment was right for Skip's technique, Art's for his; but it seemed to Bruce, as bowman in Skip's canoe, that Skip was the better canoeist because the green canoe had not swamped and Art's grey canoe had.

We stopped early that afternoon to unpack and dry out the provisions from the grey canoe; and while we waited, Skip took the opportunity to check our supplies once again. At dinner, he announced that we had consumed more sugar after going on Art's "honor system" than we had before. Joe's realism had unfortunately proven correct. Skip scowled at Joe and me, and asked what we planned to do about the situation. Tired of feeling guilty, I supported Joe in vigorously demanding that the remaining sugar be divided six ways so that everyone could look after his own.

Peter Franck, as the third sternman, stood aside and said nothing.

Bruce turned the question back to Skip, but Skip side-stepped the issue and expressed no opinion as usual.

Art sat in the background by the fire sipping his tea. Finally, he said, "It won't work, we have nothing to put the sugar in if we divide it up."

"W-w-we have s-s-six empty j-j-jam tins." Peter said. "I-I-I have b-b-been saving th-th-them."

There was a long silence.

"We tried it Art's way, and it didn't work," Bruce said, addressing Skip and ignoring Art. "It's only fair now that he try it our way."

"Put it to a vote," Joe demanded, his dark eyes flashing.

The vote was four to one, with Skip abstaining. Skip turned and looked at Art.

Art looked down: "Soon we will all have our own little fires on the tundra, and if anyone comes near, we will growl," he said.

I laughed; but Skip did not find the situation so amusing, and he glowered at me.

Bruce continued to look at Skip expectantly. Finally Skip agreed to go along with the demands of the United Bowmen's Association, as supported by Peter Franck.

To add insult to injury, Bruce suggested that Skip be the one to divide up the remaining sugar. "We trust *you*, Skip," he said pointedly.

When Skip nodded his agreement, Art stood up and left the campfire.

A rainbow circled the sky, and the ends met in the river at our feet. While we squabbled, the natural world around us was both beautiful and serene.

photo credit Arthur Moffatt

Skip Pessl

Chapter Ten
Fish Scales

The following morning, Art arose early, which was unusual for him. He talked with Skip while Skip cooked breakfast. After the meal, Art explained to us all that he had not wanted to "play the sergeant:" but if that was what we wanted, the expedition would be run more militaristically in the future.

We cheered. It was just what we wanted. We scurried about packing the canoes and launched them into the river in record time.

At lunch, Skip divided up the sugar and gave us each our week's supply in the empty jam tins which Peter provided. We clutched our sugar cans firmly to our capitalistic little breasts; every one did, that is, but Art. Art left his behind, and Skip had to carry it for him.

The rapids were bad, and the weather turned wet and stormy before the day was through. The following day, we continued down the river, but we got drenching wet from the rain and the spray off the rapids. The temperature was near freezing, and we bowmen shivered and kicked rocks to warm our feet as we waited for the sternmen to return from scouting the rapids ahead.

Later that afternoon, Art concluded that the rapids were better portaged than shot, on account of the weather; he decided to make camp early so that we would have time to catch some fish for dinner. Bruce, Pete, and Skip brought in fifteen fish of a species that was different from the delicious lake trout. Bruce thought they might be "grayling." At any rate, unlike lake trout, they had scales.

Early in the trip, I had volunteered to clean any fish caught, and to dress any game shot; so they handed me the fish, and I gutted and scaled them and handed them to Art, who tossed them in the pot of boiling water. But the fish had been slippery and I had been in too much of a hurry.

The fish were delicious, but dinner was ruined because everyone was soon spitting out fish scales. My fellow bowmen made a joke about it, but Skip took the opportunity to point out my lack of "group consideration and altruistic behavior." I retired to my tent and wrote in my journal a diatribe against self-righteous "altruists" in general and Skip in particular.

Ten days earlier, back on the Height of Land, I had become embroiled in one of many arguments with Skip. Skip had given me one of his "group consideration and altruistic behavior" lectures with appropriate disapproving looks. Though he and I were the same age, we were very different: unlike me, he had done everything right in his life.

I had been defending the position of André Gide, an author I had read while in the Army; namely, that a self-righteous hero capable of gratuitous goodness is equally capable of blowing up school buses in the name of God. Better to be openly selfish than self-righteous.

I went on to point out to Skip that, in *Lafcadio's Adventures*, Gide's saintly hero turns out to be a psychopathic killer. I looked pointedly at him as if to say "underneath that altruistic exterior of yours lies a psychopath."

Skip glowered at me.

I glowered at Skip.

Of course, Gide was a gay writer of fiction intent on anti-clerical propaganda, and his writing had little or no relevance to our present situation; but I felt as if I had just proven my case against Skip in a court of law, and I was appropriately indignant.

Skip and I spent a lot of time glowering at one another. Art just sat on a rock, as usual; he quietly sipped his evening tea and said nothing.

photo credit George Luste
Point of no return.

Chapter Eleven
Point of No Return

We launched our canoes at the foot of the rapids the next morning and continued down the river until the current slowed and the water widened into another lake. We did not follow the shore because it was very bleak, a heap of boulders denuded of vegetation with green lichen eking a meagre existence from the rocks. The glacier had shovelled the dirt off this moraine about 10,000 years ago, and nothing much had taken root on it since. That evening we camped on an island in the middle of the lake. There was a clump of stunted black spruce clinging precariously to the glacial till in a protected valley by the shore; and on a hill, the bleached bones of a caribou lay on the moss.

Skip handed Bruce a pack from their green canoe, and Bruce carried it to a dry spot on the hill. "Say Skip, is it all right if I take a pee?" Bruce hesitantly asked.

"Oh, for God's sake, Bruce, please do!" Skip replied.

Everyone laughed but Bruce. Bruce seemed puzzled. He adored Skip. He tried to emulate Skip.

He had always extolled Skip's virtues in discussions, and he wished Skip were leader instead of Art. Now Skip seemed annoyed when all Bruce had asked was permission to urinate. Bruce sauntered over to a patch of stunted spruce trees, his head down, his shoulders bent over in a slouch as if his head were too heavy for his shoulders to carry.

Bruce had always asked a lot of questions. He seemed to need permission for everything he did, no matter how trivial. At first, he had asked Art for permission; but Art did not like telling anyone what to do, and so Bruce had turned to Skip. Initially, Skip seemed to be flattered that Bruce had chosen him over Art as his mentor; but ever since Bruce had set Skip up to betray Art with the "we trust you, Skip" comment, Skip had become annoyed at his disciple.

What Bruce knew, being Skip's tentmate, was that Skip, like the rest of us, believed he could run the expedition better than Art. Skip had made the mistake of letting Bruce read his diary. Bruce had reported the subversive passages to the United Bowmen's Association and had taken upon himself the role of Lady MacBeth; but Skip had even less desire to be the instrument of our rebellion than to be "second-in-command" to Art. Caught in a box, Skip was getting increasingly annoyed at Bruce, at the United Bowmen's Association, at Art, and at everything else connected with the expedition. The social cohesion, so strong in the beginning of the trip, was disintegrating rapidly with every passing day.

"Turning and turning in the widening gyre / The falcon cannot hear the falconer," as William Butler

Yeats so presciently wrote. "Things fall apart; the centre cannot hold; / Mere anarchy is loosed upon the world...."

Before coming on the trip, particularly when I had been on guard duty in the Army, I used to while away the midnight hours memorizing poetry. Guard duty is a deeply spiritual experience. Guards do not have anything to do, they simply have to stay awake. The best way to stay awake is to keep walking; but in as much as guards have no physical destination, they must create a spiritual destination, or the meaning of life disintegrates in the silence of the midnight bleakness.

John Keat's poem, "La Belle Dame Sans Merci," had become my favorite to memorize while sauntering around the motor pool trying desultorily to prevent my buddies from transferring gas from Army trucks to their own dilapidated vehicles so as to be able to drive to their girl friends on the weekends.

"Oh what can ail thee, Knight at arms, / Alone and palely loitering? / The sedge is withered from the lake, / And no birds sing." Keats had something else in mind for his knight-at-arms than guarding a motor pool; but his lyrical lines took me off to a distant world, half asleep while still on my feet, plodding around the idle trucks. And now, forty days in the wilderness, another poem kept returning to my consciousness, one not so much lyrical as prophetic. "The blood-dimmed tide is loosed, and everywhere / The ceremony of innocence is drowned."

The wind and rain held us prisoner on the island for two days. Art caught a lake trout that was almost as large as he was. It slipped off his hook near shore and almost got away; but Art, with amazing agility, jumped into the lake, embraced the fish in both arms, and flipped it onto dry land before it could wriggle to freedom.

In a Buddhist koan, the master says: "A fish saved my life once."
The disciple says: "How could a fish save your life?"
The master replies: "I ate it."

Although we feasted on Art's fish for the next two days, a civilized supermarket still seemed preferable to me.

In the afternoon of the second day on the island, I took a canoe out on the lake by myself to prove to Art that it would be possible to load up and continue on our way, but Art ignored the suggestion. After dinner that evening, though, he became very sombre and asked us if we wanted to turn around and go back to civilization the safe way, back through the outpost at Stony Rapids.

He elaborated on what we already knew: at our current rate of travel we no longer carried enough food in our canoes to reach the outpost at Baker Lake. Our progress across the Barrens had been slower than he had anticipated, so that we were in danger of being trapped by freeze-up as well as by hunger.

Our only hope of survival lay in living off the land. If we were lucky to run across a herd of migrating caribou, we would probably survive: if not, we should expect the same fate as Hornby, Adlard and Christian, death by starvation.

Even though the outpost at Baker Lake was still about twice as far away as the outpost at Stony Rapids, another day or two on the river and we would lose the option of turning back. The swiftness of the current and the violence of the rapids had already made difficult our line of retreat. We would soon be trapped in both directions. Art was very sombre.

I listened intently to what Art was telling us, but I was desperate to continue on; and in the end we all voted to take our chances.

"O.K.," Art said. "I just wanted to make sure everyone understands the risks."

The light drizzle persisted through the night; we rose early, hurried through breakfast, and packed the canoes; everyone hurried, that is, but Art, who remained on the hill by the breakfast fire sipping his tea as if he were having second thoughts. "The best lack all conviction, while the worst / Are full of passionate intensity."

It was my day to wash the dishes; and, when I had finished, I brought the two-gallon oatmeal pot back from the lake full of water and stood facing Art. He looked at me with a friendly expression on his face.

The others were scurrying about loading the canoes down by the lake. A light rain was falling, as it had been for the previous two days. There was no danger of our campfire starting a forest fire on this island because there was no forest, only a few stunted spruce trees down in a protected valley by the lake; but I carried the oatmeal bucket back up the hill anyway, full of water.

With a frown on my face, I stared at Art while he smiled at me. He seemed to understand the place I had arrived at spiritually; but when I studied his face, I was totally puzzled. If we were truly in so much danger, why was he not down with the others rushing about? If there was no danger, what was the meaning of his frightening speech the night before? Had he just been trying to scare us so that we would stop bickering and work together once again?

Or did he really want to turn back and go home the safe way to his wife and children?

Although I had some concern about the dangers which lay ahead, I was much more afraid that Art had changed his mind about continuing on. I wanted to be born again. I believed that the new-me was waiting around a bend in the river ahead. The last verse of Yeats's "The Second Coming" kept churning through my mind: "Surely some revelation is at hand; / Surely the Second Coming is at hand."

I was absolutely determined that my hour must come round at last. Already I had begun to feel my new identity unfolding within me, like a beetle being transmuted into a dragonfly.

The Second Coming! Hardly are those words out
When a vast image out of *Spiritus Mundi*

Troubles my sight: somewhere in sands of the
desert
A shape with lion body and the head of a man,
A gaze blank and pitiless as the sun,
Is moving its slow thighs, while all about it
Reel shadows of the indignant desert birds.

I feared now only one thing, that Art would
change his mind and imprison me spiritually in my
beetle-shell for eternity.
Why was he smiling at me?

In Medieval times, theologians had divided life
into four passages, childhood, youth, middle age, and
old age: each passage in the voyage to wisdom lasted
eighteen years, with the final destination at death
being the City of God. In modern civilization, on the
other hand, life is seen more as a physical journey
through the Gross Domestic Product to the morgue.
Of course, the divisions in the passages of life
are not, in practice, as rigid as Medieval theory. Wise
even in childhood, Saint Anthony made the
pilgrimage to the heavenly kingdom at eighteen; but
most of us are less successful in our spiritual journey.
We prefer the seven deadly sins of civilization
(avarice, envy, gluttony, lust, sloth, anger and pride)
to the inner peace of a spiritual life. We scratch, we
pinch, we claw our way through the rat race,
accumulating what we consider to be our rightful
portion of the Gross Domestic Product; and it is not
until we lie on our death beds that we realize the
truth — today's garbage dumps were yesterday's gross

domestic products, and so are we. Our children look on our monuments with bewilderment.

At twenty-two, I should already have passed from childhood into youth, passed from dependency to independency, passed, in William Blake's poetic imagery, from lamb to tiger; but I had lingered in childhood. Art, on the other hand, had reached the City of God early in life. Like so many veterans, he had viewed his tombstone from the other side of paradise before his time was up. He had become wise; but while he was wise, he was also thirty-six, married, with a family to support. He could see the futility of the rat race, the meaninglessness of the quest for gold, the vanity of planting flags on Everest, and the beauty of the wilderness; but he also had to feed his family, and leading a spiritual journey into the wilderness was not the best way to do it. At thirty-six, making the agonizing passage from youth to middle age, Art missed his wife and children.

Art looked into my eyes and seemed to understand the station at which I had arrived in my pilgrimage; but when I looked into his eyes, I understood nothing of his inner turmoil, because he had travelled much further on the spiritual journey. I understood only that if he decided to turn around and go home, I would be trapped half way through my own transmutation and remain a child forever.

The darkness drops again...;

We had spent forty days fasting in the wilderness together, he and I; but I had not reached his level of understanding.

> ... but now I know
> That twenty centuries of stony sleep
> Were vexed to nightmare by a rocking cradle
> And what rough beast, its hour come round at last,
> Slouches towards Bethlehem to be born?

At any rate, some rough beast rose up in me and dumped the pot of water on the campfire. The flames sizzled, steamed, spat at Art and died. Art looked at me. This rough beast scowled back at him. Resignedly, he arose and walked down the hill to join the others. After forty days in the wilderness, I had not been transformed into Jesus Christ, rather into something more like Yeats's rough beast with its gaze "blank and pitiless as the sun."

The last bit of warmth on that cold, wet tundra died: and soon Art would die as well, never to return to his wife and children, nor complete that final passage of life — or had he completed it already?

photo credit Richard Irwin

Caribou

Chapter Twelve
Caribou

Caribou!" I exclaimed in a whispered yell. A caribou with great antlers arched to the sky was standing on top of a hill overlooking the Dubawnt River. Art had already stopped paddling; he turned towards shore, stepped out of his canoe and splashed onto the bank, movie camera in hand.

"Stay by the canoes!" he whispered hoarsely at us bowmen as he bounded up the hill. Skip, with a still camera, followed him cautiously at a distance, and so did Peter Franck.

"If he doesn't let us shoot it, what will we do?" Bruce asked Joe.

"I'll use my rifle on Art," Joe replied. "You use yours on the caribou."

We bowmen sat on the moss and waited. The majestic caribou stood sentinel for a long time, then suddenly it jumped into the air and pranced out of sight behind a distant hill.

When the sternmen returned, we continued down the river. Upon rounding a bend, we saw hundreds of caribou, then thousands more. They were grazing on the hills, resting by the river. Some pranced away when they saw us coming, others did not bother to get to their feet. They lay on the bank chewing their cud lethargically and watched us pass.

Art continued to paddle downstream while our mouths drooled. Eventually he pulled in to shore to make camp. When Bruce and Joe reached for their rifles, Art said he would accompany them to film the hunt. Bruce and Joe looked at each other quizzically, but said nothing. There were so many caribou, it was difficult to believe that Art would be able to protect them all.

After the hunters left camp, Skip and I tried to lasso a caribou that had wandered into camp. It seemed more puzzled by our antics than afraid. Eventually it swam the river and grazed on the far side.

The hunters returned to lead me to their kill. I slit the belly, rolled up my sleeves and reached in through the warm intestines to remove the heart and liver. The words I had heard repeated so frequently at Communion in the Chapel at Groton rang in my ears: "This is my body and blood which is given for you, eat, drink in remembrance of me." We carried the butchered caribou back to camp and that evening gratefully ate forty-two steaks.

There is a Buddhist joke about an old man and his friend the rabbit. The rabbit saw that the old man was hungry and so jumped into the fire to roast itself, and the old man saw that the rabbit was Buddha. As I filled my hungry belly, I saw the roasted caribou as Buddha, as Jesus Christ, as the symbol of everything sacred in the world. It had died for me as it had died for the others, Art included.

I had met this God before at the supermarket, wrapped in cellophane in the form of eviscerated chickens, minced hamburger and the like, the remains of animals which had also sacrificed their lives; but they had seemed to me more like meat than God.

Backwards along the path of enlightenment, Art had been carrying us kicking and screaming. He had led us back from the modern supermarket down the long spiritual path to the world of the Lascaux caves.

There is a picture in those caves of France, painted twenty thousand years ago, of a shaman dressed in caribou fur with arms and legs raised like a caribou prancing. I wanted to dress like a caribou and prance about also. I wanted to turn the caribou into me by eating it, and I wanted to turn me into a caribou so that I would no longer be an alien stranger in this beautiful wilderness.

Art's method of educating us had been very different from the methods by which I was educated at Groton, Harvard, and in the United States Army. At Groton and Harvard, I had been trained to become part of the richest oligarchy in world history. In the Army, I had been trained to be part of the most powerful military force in world history. But Art's method was completely different. He waited for the wilderness to do the educating.

What Art had understood, and what we had not, is that God is not he who kills and eats, but that which is killed and is eaten. If one waits around in the Garden of Eden long enough, either one will die, or one will begin to feel some spirit carrying one to a place of inner peace as if one has returned to one's spiritual home. After forty days of fasting in the wilderness, I could see God more clearly now prancing about the hills.

At Groton, we boys could be seen each Sunday evening rushing out of Chapel to "Hundred House" where dinner was served at long tables. Masters sat at each end, and the entire dining room was surveyed from an elevated head table with a large bay window behind it. When the Reverend John Crocker, jr. ("the Reverend Jesus Christ, jr." as we called the Headmaster) looked down from the head table, he could see all the boys. When the boys looked up, what they saw was the blinding light of the sun forming a halo behind his head. Groton was the mural upon which my life had been painted.

One Sunday after Evensong, the Reverend John Crocker, jr. admonished us for rushing out of Chapel to dinner. "So much of life is spent running after those things that are really not worth running after," he had mused in that philosophical manner of his, and seemed puzzled when we burst out laughing.

Before meals, two hundred boys stood behind their chairs silently waiting for grace. "Bless, O Lord, this food to our use, and us to thy service."

As I butchered and ate the late Jesus Christ in the form of a caribou, part of the Christian liturgy ("this is my body and blood which is given for you") came back to me; but the Groton school grace seemed more puzzling. For in that benediction lay an uneasy mix of service and use. As the caribou became my body, its spirit began an argument in my heart against the disharmony of my boyhood grace.

Groton had been founded in the previous century by the Reverend Endicott Peabody for the moral improvement of the sons of the rich. F o r the privilege of having our morals improved and for the ancillary benefit of getting us out from underfoot, my parents, or rather my great uncle, George Bird Grinnell, had paid Groton major dollars. George Bird Grinnell had followed a slightly different path than my other relatives; he appears to have been interested in other things besides making money. He founded the Audubon Society, the American Museum of Natural History, and the magazine *Field and Stream*. He went out West to live with the Indians and wrote forty books attempting to preserve their stories and their culture. He worked hard to restore to them the lands my other relatives were stealing from them to build railroads across the nation; and before he died, the Blackfoot Nation made him Honorary Chief. He was also a close friend of President Theodore Roosevelt and together they founded Yellowstone National Park and Glacier National Park, where Grinnell Glacier and Grinnell Mountain were named in his honor. He had taken my father out West to meet the Indians, but why he paid my way through Groton is not so clear to me. Groton trained my soul to march, but the caribou taught it to dance. I could not march and dance at the same time.

The Reverend Endicott Peabody had modeled Groton after Eton and Harrow, the boarding schools in England which trained British aristocrats to act like patronizing snots. Eton and Harrow, in turn, had been modeled after the schools of the Jesuits. The Groton school prayer: "Teach us, O Lord, to give and not to count the cost, to seek and not to hope to find, to labor and not to ask for any reward save that of knowing that we do thy will," was plagiarized and abridged by Peabody (without acknowledgement) directly from Saint Ignatius Loyola, the founder of the Society of Jesus. It has never been clear to me whether we were being trained to follow Jesus or to take over theAmerican Empire. The Grotonian creed rested like a burden in my arms, and its legacy became the voyage I could not complete.

The Groton graduate who is best known around the world is Franklin Delano Roosevelt, President of the United States from 1933 to 1945. Other Grotonians during that time had already infiltrated the Senate, the State Department, and a large number of investment banking firms including my father's. (Jimmy Roosevelt, Franklin's son, was a "junior" partner in my father's investment banking firm.)

Once in power, Grotonians created the most powerful war machine the world had ever seen. Before and during the Second World War, Roosevelt secretly appropriated from Congress two billion dollars to mass-produce nuclear weapons.

Roosevelt is frequently portrayed as a friend of the poor, and then again so was Hitler; but there was a darker side to both their administrations. Under the guise of aid to "farmers," Roosevelt bankrupted the homesteaders and enriched the rich. Today in America, there are no homesteaders left, and Jeffersonian democracy is dead.

When boys reach the "Sixth Form" at Groton, they receive a dark blue Groton blazer which has the Groton crest over the left breast pocket with the words "cui servire est regnare" embroidered in gold on a crimson, silver and black background. If you ask a Grotonian what the words means, he will recite: "whom to serve is perfect freedom." If you read Latin, on the other hand, you will know what the words really mean: "whom to serve is to rule." Who this "whom" is that we were supposed to be serving has remained enigmatic to me these past forty years.

In the Middle Ages, the serfs had handed over a third of their produce to the Lords of the Manor. Today, the few remaining family farmers hand over more than 90% of their produce to the Lords of Wall Street. At the time of the American Revolution, 72% of the population had worked their own farms and were free of debt. Today less than 2% of the population own their own farms, and 85% of the people are up to their ears in debt. The average farmer today works longer hours than a Medieval serf and turns over a larger portion of his or her produce to the new Lords in the form of interest on their bank loans. Roosevelt called this his "New

Deal." If you are up to your ears in debt and have been dispossessed of American land, you have us Grotonians to thank.

Or perhaps you don't. There are many reasons for the bankruptcy of Jeffersonian democracy. Groton and Roosevelt's "New Deal" are not the only culprits, but we Grotonians certainly did not reverse the trend. Once the American people had been driven off the land into the cities under the guise of "farm aid," they had to borrow money to buy a home, a car, food. Those that could not afford to buy a house or car or food became dependent on the Government, which borrowed the money for them. The poor got poorer, the middle class got taxed to desperation, and Grotonians, along with other bankers, had their hands outstretched collecting interest on the debt.

Discipline at Groton had been strict. If a First Former showed disrespect to a Sixth Former, he was summarily tossed down the second floor dust chute. More severe cases of disrespect were punished by "pumping." There was only one bathtub at Groton and it was not used for bathing. (We washed in tin basins). The disrespectful lower Former was ordered into the Senior Prefect's office, then taken to the bathtub, where he was "pumped." Before the boy drowned, he was rushed over to the infirmary and pumped out. This practice had to be discontinued when irate parents of one boy threatened to bring charges of attempted murder against the Senior Prefect who had pumped him, and likewise the practice of tossing disrespectful lower Formers down the second floor dust chute was also discontinued because of broken bones; but both practices had been in use to enforce discipline when Franklin Delano Roosevelt and my father attended Groton. Beneath the angelic guise of Christianity lay the reality of ruthless submission to the hierarchy.

Despite Japanese enquiries about terms of peace more than a month before Hiroshima and Nagasaki were vaporized, altimeters were attached to the uranium and plutonium bombs so as to detonate them in a fashion and at a time of day causing the maximum loss of life. Roosevelt had died before the bombs were dropped, but his quest for world power carried the atom bomb project to fruition.

Although Admiral Nimitz and General Eisenhower favored replying to the Japanese overtures to peace and were opposed to dropping the bombs, they were overruled; and on the morning of August 6th, 1945, 9,172 Japanese children on their way to school went down the dust chute in Hiroshima, to say nothing of 70,000 Japanese civilians. All told, about 400,000 Japanese people died from the two bombs, the explosions, the fires, and the radiation burns afterwards: about twenty times the number of people killed by all German bombs dropped on London during the Second World War.

O merciful Father... grant that we receiving these thy creatures... in remembrance of his death and passion, may be partakers of his most blessed Body and

Blood, who in the same night that he was betrayed took Bread, and when he had given thanks, he brake and gave it to his disciples, saying, Take, eat, this is my Body which is given for you....

As I ate the caribou, I began to feel "lucky," as an old trapper once said, although the word I would have chosen was more like "grateful:" grateful that this majestic and beautiful creature had sacrificed its life that I might live.

My understanding of truth and beauty was not as profound as Art's, but I was beginning to travel down the same path he had travelled by walking away from the "corridors of power" to a place of inner peace in the wilderness — a peace that all the order of Groton could not bestow upon my father. For him, "perfect freedom" was gained in the cry of a gunshot, a numb rapid sound that was the only expression his anguish about "whom to serve" ever took.

My father had not been the first Grotonian to commit suicide, nor would he be the last. Another Grotonian, John Bigelow, who was destined to become my future father-in-law, had escaped into the Army during the Second World War, where he attempted to get himself killed in battle. He only succeeded in becoming a hero, in receiving a battlefield commission, and in being promoted to Major. After the war, he tried to escape into the mountains of Wyoming, where he found a job as a primary school teacher. He was immensely popular with his students and drank himself to death in the wee hours of the morning. Perhaps Roosevelt, like my father, and like my father-in-law, had only been trying to do his best. By Groton standards that was not good enough.

The Catholic Church is more realistic: either become a saint, or raise a family, or rule an Empire, but not all three at once.

When I was a Sixth Former at Groton, I had fallen in love. Groton was designed like a monastery, but occasionally a visiting parent would bring along the sister of one of the boys to the school; and such an event occurred in the Spring of my final year.

Generally boys in the upper Forms did not converse with boys in the lower Forms; but exceptions were made in athletics because good athletes could be promoted out of the Clubs onto the Varsity teams, even if they were not in the Sixth Form. Such was the case with John Parkinson.

In a football huddle, the quarterback says words like: "Two-three on four." We clap our hands, line up, and, on the count of four, crash into one another. In male circles, this passes for intimacy.

"Two" refers to the left half-back, "three" to the slot off-tackle on the left side of the line, and "four" to the count when the ball is snapped. Conversations in a football huddle tend to be brief. Intimacy consists of hitting the man with the ball hard enough so that he is not eager to get up.

I was the number "Two" back and had found myself one year under one of these pile-ups with a broken arm, in another year with a dislocated knee, and during a third year in an intimate embrace with John Parkinson.

In the Spring of my final year at Groton, John's mother and sister came to visit and were invited to join us at lunch by the Headmaster. They were waiting outside the dining hall, surrounded by silently staring male adolescents. The Masters were all delayed in a Faculty meeting: as a Sixth Former, I had the duty to make them feel welcome, in the absence of any Masters. I walked over to them, introduced myself, and tried to carry on a conversation.

The doors to the dinning room opened, the boys flooded in to stand behind their chairs waiting for the Headmaster to arrive and say grace so they could eat; but neither he nor any of the other Masters appeared.

I stayed with the Parkinsons until finally the Faculty meeting was over, and the Headmaster arrived with apologies. He led them up to the Head Table, situated on the platform in front of the large bay window from which all light and truth was disseminated throughout the dinning room. Below two hundred adolescent males stood silently at their places.

I found an empty place at the center of the Fourth Form table, and after grace, sat down. After grace, everyone was allowed to speak, and soon the dining hall was full of chatter and of clanging dishes, but suddenly there was total silence. Zaidee Parkinson, John's seventeen year old, younger sister, in defiance of all protocol, had left the Head Table and was crossing through the lower dining room towards me. Every male eye was upon her. The next generation of the rigid Groton hierarchy which ruled the American Empire was beginning to crumble at the groin with every step she took.

Her leaving the Head Table was a direct insult to the Headmaster, and at Groton no one ever insulted the Headmaster. Zaidee's father and brother were Grotonians; she knew the rules, but she was no more intimidated by the Reverend "Jesus Christ jr.", who looked alternately bemused and perplexed, than by any other male. If the Reverend John Crocker was not going to be polite enough to invite me to sit with her and her mother at the Head Table when I had been kind enough to keep them company while waiting for him to get out of his Faculty meeting, she was not going to be so rude as to allow me to sit alone at the Fourth Form table. I stood up, pulled out a chair for her and, by the end of lunch, was hopelessly in love.

I did not get to see much of Zaidee for another year or so. By that time, I had graduated from Groton and had managed to get myself thrown out of Harvard (not as easy as it may sound). I had passed the courses of the Navy Reserve Officers Training Corps, despite my best efforts — but nothing else. The Navy could not believe that anyone smart enough to get into Harvard could be stupid enough to flunk the Navy, but other Professors had been more realistic.

Having received some unflattering letters from the Administration, I left Harvard and went home.

My father had just committed suicide, and so out of compassion for me, the Dean of Students at Harvard invited me back. My father had gone to Harvard. My mother's father had gone to Harvard and had become a Professor of Economics there. Like Groton, Harvard tries to be a family, even if it is a family of power-happy rich snots. But although I loved my father, I did not want to follow in his footsteps. I took up painting instead.

In the mornings, I painted a mural up the stairs from the third to the fourth floor in my family's house in New York City. It was the representation of an allegorical journey from the Garden of Eden to Buddhist Nirvana with the rise and fall of Empires depicted in the background. (A psychiatrist, who shortly thereafter purchased the house, took a second, more professional, look at me after seeing that mural.)

In the afternoons, I visited Zaidee in her studio. She was studying at the Juliard School of Music to be a concert pianist. I loved her music, and I loved her, and she loved Peter Mathieson of the *Paris Review*. He was too busy jetting over to Paris to spend much time with her and so she was glad for my company. When she was tired of practising the piano, we would go for walks in Central Park and talk of Rilke and poems of sweet sadness while the cherry blossoms fell.

George Plympton, one of the editors of the *Paris Review*, liked to festoon his armchairs with *Vogue* models. Zaidee took me to one of his parties, and I approached an elegant girl without much meat on her bones while Zaidee was busy elsewhere with Peter

110

Mathieson. The conversation was brief. The model looked at me as if I were an interesting breed of cockroach. A few days later, Zaidee took me to a dance and bet me ten dollars that I could not take to bed the Accessories Editor of *Vogue*, whom she pointed out to me. It was a bet that neither I nor anyone else could possibly lose, which is undoubtedly why she made it; but it was poor consolation for my unrequited love of her. The affair was a brief one. I retired to the woods of New Hampshire and kept company with the porcupines and woodchucks, who were kind enough to feed me: and from there I went to the Army and then to the Arctic.

In the beginning of the trip, the women of my dreams resembled Zaidee and the *Vogue* model; there was not much meat on their bones. As the trip progressed, and as I became more hungry, the women of my dreams filled out and began serving me more food than sex. Then the women dropped out altogether, and I just dreamed of food.

While we consumed forty-two caribou steaks that evening, there was a reverential hush. Maybe we were just too busy stuffing our mouths to talk, but the words still ring in my ears: "This is my body and blood which is given for you; eat, drink in remembrance of me." The miracle of transubstantiation was taking place inside my belly, and also in my soul.

Art had taken me to a place where I could love the God of the caribou more than I loved the wealth and security of the American Empire, even more than I loved Zaidee.

photo credit Robert Herendeen

Tundra Time

Chapter Thirteen
Tundra Time

Full bellies, skies of purest blue, warm sun, and a flat calm lake; at supper, a few days after we had killed our first caribou, Joe had said that he was bored. He had come on the trip to do some writing, but there was nothing to write about. All we ever did was eat, portage, paddle and squabble.

Art replied that if Hemingway could create a major literary masterpiece describing a weekend fishing trip in Spain, there must be something interesting to write about.

Joe grunted. He was not the only one who felt bored. At the beginning of the trip, we had imagined excitement, danger and heroic acts of courage. The reality had turned out differently. We had discovered black flies in the wilderness, irritation in one another, and pettiness in ourselves. These were not the stuff of epic poems to be sung through the ages celebrating our everlasting glory. Better to write nothing at all than to tell the truth about this expedition.

At lunch that day, we had our usual squabble about what time it was. My watch read 1:30, indicating that lunch was long overdue. Art's watch read 11:43, indicating that it was not yet time for lunch.

A couple of weeks earlier, Art had settled the schedule dispute by picking up his paddle and continuing down the lake. On the surface, the bowmen's strike had been broken when we followed him; but underneath, the split remained, and we bowmen exacerbated that split by insisting that my watch told the "correct" time.

At the beginning of the trip, we had set our watches to "Moffatt Time;" but one by one, all the watches had broken down except Art's and mine. The discrepancy between them had reached nearly two hours and was growing larger with every passing day. Earlier in the trip, I would have reset my watch to agree with his in deference to his position as our leader; but by the time the United Bowmen's Association had been formed, I could no longer believe that his watch was more accurate than mine, and neither could my fellow bowmen. They had quickly converted to "George's Time," while the sternmen remained on "Moffatt Time." Whenever anyone asked if it were time for lunch, he had to specify whose time he wanted the answer in.

The discussions over lunchtime turned out to be Academic. As Art had mentioned in the beginning of the trip, "he who controls the food, controls the men." He kept the luncheon pack in front of him in his canoe, so we continued to eat lunch on "Moffatt Time" whether we liked it or not; but our civilized food was running thin and so was the time on Moffatt's watch.

The majority of our tundra food was now coming from us bowmen who possessed the rifles, and I had spent a great deal more money on my watch than Art had on his.

About a week after killing the first caribou, there was nothing left of it but bones. Art boiled up the skeleton into a delicious soup, and we all voted to take a holiday to kill another. Everyone voted to take a holiday, that is, but Peter Franck.

While Bruce went hunting, Skip, Joe and Art picked blueberries; and that afternoon, Art baked up a delicious blueberry "Johnny Cake" in his reflector oven. We feasted that night on caribou soup, Johnny Cake, some of the dehydrated mashed potatoes Art had brought along for celebrations such as this, and freshly butchered caribou steaks. Everyone was happy. The feeling around the campfire was much as it had been early in the trip, when we all had had full bellies and all had felt good about Art.

To celebrate the return of good times, I tried to remember some old Army jokes. They fell flat, but Art's old jokes were better received.

"Two cavalry officers were overheard talking on a train. The first one said: 'I heard old Chomedley was cashiered.'

'Oh, what for?'

'Sexual intercourse with his horse.'

'Was it a mare?'

'Oh yes, nothing queer about old Chomedley'."

We all laughed, but I think Art's jokes were even more stale than mine. They had either been recycled from the First World War or from the days when his father had worked tending the horses of Art's wealthy patron.

With encouragement from us, he told another.

"An Indian Chief goes to a white man's doctor, complaining about a pain in his stomach. The doctor prescribes a laxative and tells the Chief to come back the next day.

'Move?' the Doctor asks, on the next day.

The Indian shakes his head, and the doctor prescribes more laxative. The following day, the Indian returns.

'Move?'

The Indian shakes his head. More laxatives are prescribed.

'Move?'

'Had to,' the Indian replies. 'Tepee full of shit'."

Indians and white men do not always speak the same language. We spoke to Art in the language of the American Empire. Art tried his best to reply in the language of the Indians. The result was that our tepees had all filled with shit.

After dinner, in the spirit of reconciliation and full bellies, we decided to come to an agreement about the time. We all sat around studying the sunset and joking about our differences. The date was August 12th, and the sun set much further to the south than it had when we had arrived at Stony Rapids during the Summer Solstice, a month and a half ago. Then the sun had just dipped below the northern horizon, where it had glowed pink for a few hours before rising again in the northeast. Now it had migrated more to the south and the night sky was once again black.

While we waited for the sun to go down, we observed flocks of song birds flying around in circles, preparing for their migration south. Everything on the Tundra seemed to be migrating south but us.

The river seemed to be carrying us through the caribou herd in the wrong direction. We had already passed through the main herd, and only stragglers were left to hunt. The faster we paddled, the sooner we would be out of meat. It had seemed to make more sense that day to take a holiday and hunt caribou than to continue down the river. More sense, that is, to everyone but Peter.

As the sun went down, we tried to joke good-naturedly about continuing north when our food supply was heading south; but our laughter had a hollow ring to it.

Staring at the setting sun with the best of intentions, we still could not agree on which of the two watches was "right." The only thing that was clear to us was that the Autumn colors of the tundra were telling us that the time of Summer had passed.

Despite loyal support by my fellow bowmen, Art's watch that evening was the sentimental favorite: it was a cheap "dollar" watch which he had carried in his pocket on all his trips. Skip and Pete, who had been on trips before with Art, remembered it with fondness. In contrast, I had bought my watch at the

Army PX shortly before coming on the trip: it was a fine Swiss watch, modern and new. Logic and bowmen loyalty favored my watch; but sentiment, a desire to return to the good old days, and Art's blueberry Johnny Cake had done much to sway public opinion in his favor.

One by one, we turned into our sleeping bags. Art lingered by the fire.

> August 12th: ... Cold now, but I love these evenings alone by the fire, late at night and early in the morning. I smoke, drink tea, think of home, Carol, Creigh and Debbo, of my study, and the children there with me when I get back, and the stories I'll tell about my adventures in the north — shooting rapids, and the time I saw the wolves, white ones, and the caribou and moose and fish and birds. Already, as 2 A.M. approaches, the fog grows lighter, and dawn approaches. We may move tomorrow when the fog lifts. It might be wise to get some sleep.

When I awoke the next morning, I noticed that the hands of my watch were pointing at five minutes to twelve. I held it to my ear and heard nothing. I shook it; the hands moved a bit, and then stopped. At breakfast, I was silent.

Art was silent also. Finally Joe asked us what time it was. Art and I continued to eat our oatmeal.

Everyone looked back and forth at us. At last, Art mumbled that his watch had stopped in the night.

It suddenly occurred to me that I had forgotten to wind mine. I wound it, and it began to tick: but now no one knew what time it "really" was. We looked at the dawning sun and made guesses: but from that day on, our schedule was not based on "Moffatt Time," nor "George's Time," but on "Tundra Time."

photo credit Robert Herendeen
Studying the rapids.
The lower gorge exiting Dubawnt Lake
which we did not shoot.

Chapter Fourteen
The Widening Gyre

One... two... three... four!.. FIVE! Bruce's voice became more indignant with every spoonful of oatmeal Art dished into his pannikin. The rest of us were standing around silently trying not to move. Every time I lifted my spoon to my mouth, rain ran down the back of my neck into my shirt. I was trying to figure out which was more uncomfortable: to keep my neck straight and raise my arm, or to leave my arm low and bend my head. The rain managed to get down my neck either way. Water was also dripping off the hem of my poncho, which was another good reason not to move. When I moved, it ran into my boots.

Ever since Bruce had become the major source of our food supply, he had been challenging Art's authority. Today, he was counting out loud the number of spoonfuls of oatmeal Art was helping himself to in his large pannikin. Bruce was gathering evidence that Art was taking more than his share. At first, Bruce had counted silently. Today, he was counting audibly; and the count was getting louder with every spoonful Art took.

After the first hunt, Joe, who had never shot an animal before, swore he would never shoot another. Seeing the beautiful caribou die had been too painful for him, which meant that we were all dependent on Bruce for our survival: and Bruce was now stalking Art.

The date was August 15th. We had been held up by a dangerous rapids that ran through a gorge ahead. There was a high cliff on our side of the river, which made scouting the rapids difficult. After spending an afternoon scouting, Art had been unable to decide whether to portage around the gorge or to shoot it. By the end of the day, he had decided to make camp and to take a second look in the morning.

The next morning, rain squalls were lashing our tents. Art decided to wait out the storm. He thought that if the weather would co-operate, the gorge could be shot: but the weather was not co-operating. The squalls blowing up the gorge created high waves in the rapids.

We set up the kitchen tarpaulin to wait out the weather. Wild storm clouds continued to blow this way and that over beautiful hills of Autumn tundra awash in colors of orange, maroon and purple; and thus we waited four days for Art to make a decision about the gorge.

A week earlier, we had also been held up by wind and rapids. The sternmen had gone downstream to scout; and we bowmen, as usual, had been left to watch the canoes. Because the sternmen had been gone on that occasion for several hours, we bowmen had climbed up the steep bank and had made ourselves comfortable on the caribou moss with our backs leaning against a rocky ledge out of the wind. We could see the canoes below, but were not paying much attention to them.

"Say Joe, how many spoonfuls of oatmeal did you get this morning?" Bruce had asked.

"Three and half," Joe replied. "Not counting 'seconds'." Joe's appetite for oatmeal had been acquired on the trip, but Bruce's was of longer duration.

"How many did you get, George?"

"Four."

We doled our own oatmeal with a large serving spoon into standard size bowls. The unwritten rule was that we could pile as much oatmeal into our bowls as they would hold, but God help anyone who let the milk run over the edge.

After we had filled our bowls, Skip had glanced at the pot and announced how many spoonfuls we would be allowed to take for seconds. The dishwasher got the privilege of licking the pot, but as usual there was nothing left to lick.

Joe murmured words of support for Bruce's suspicions; then there was silence while Bruce and Joe inhaled deep drags of smoke from their cigarettes, and we all contemplated the nature of Art's sins.

Oatmeal was not the only issue which separated Bruce from Art. Earlier in the trip, Art had exercised his wit at the expense of "sportsmen," from which it was clear that in Art's judgment, sportsmen were to be consigned to a circle of hell below war mongers and British mountain climbers. Art was not in favor of killing animals, even when he was facing starvation; but to kill an animal for "sport" was for him too horrible to contemplate.

Bruce was a "sportsman." He had joined the expedition because of the unparalleled opportunities to fish virgin waters and to kill "game" for "sport."

At the beginning of the trip, Bruce had nodded his head in apparent agreement with everything Art or anybody else had said; but now that the expedition had become dependent on him for our meat supply, a new, more assertive Bruce had begun to appear. The "sportsman" was coming out of the closet, and the "game" he was hunting was now Art.

Bruce took a long drag on his cigarette. "Art took SEVEN!" he announced.

Leaning back against the ledge, I could hear the green canoe, the one Skip and Bruce shared, rubbing on a rock. Joe and Art had pulled their grey canoe safely out of the wash from the rapids, and Peter and I had done the same with the red canoe; but a rock was gradually digging a hole through the bottom of Skip and Bruce's green canoe.

Not content with stalking Art, Bruce also placed Peter Franck in his sights. Peter and Bruce had totally different personalities. Peter went his own way and did not seem to give a damn what people thought of him, while Bruce was the exact opposite. The old Bruce had bent over backwards not to offend anyone. He had never done anything on his own without first asking permission from Art or Skip to make sure it was all right. Earlier, Bruce had depended on Joe, me, or Skip to express his feelings for him; he had simply nodded his head in vigorous support if we said anything he approved of — but times had changed. He still seemed to want support from Joe and me, but the opinions which were now coming to the surface were his own.

Joe and I were silent. Joe was more than willing to trash Art, and I was more than willing to trash Skip; but neither one of us had anything against Pete. At worst, he minded his own business. At best, he was the hardest worker in camp; and so the conversation came to an end.

"Say, Joe, how many cigarettes have you got left?" Bruce asked, changing the subject.

Joe put his head down, mumbling something incoherent. He took a last drag on his cigarette, handing me the butt. "What about you, Bruce?"

"One tin and two cartons of 'tailor-mades'."

"Hell, Bruce! You're in great shape!" Joe exclaimed. Joe was a little self-conscious about having the largest tobacco supply in camp.

I pinched out Joe's butt, tore open the paper, and collected the strands of tobacco in an empty cigarette pack. After some serious study, I judged that I had almost enough tobacco for a cigarette. Joe was the most generous member of the expedition with his cigarette butts, for which I was deeply grateful. I kept my eye on Bruce. With this new assertive mood he was in, I was afraid he would flick his butt away.

"How much tobacco has Art got?" Bruce asked.

"Just one more tin." As Art's bowman and tentmate, Joe had insider information.

"When Art runs out of tobacco, that's when this expedition is really going to get a move on," Bruce said.

Joe chuckled.

Bruce took a deep drag, burned his lips and flicked his butt vehemently towards the river. I jumped down the cliff and caught it before it hit the water.

"Sorry, George," Bruce said.

"That's O.K. Bruce," I replied, not wanting to alienate my second most generous supplier of tobacco.

Eventually the sternmen returned with blueberry stains on their fingers and lips. They had been gone about three hours, some of which had presumably been spent scouting the rapids. The wind was blowing up against the current, creating high waves; so Art had decided to make camp.

Art's solution to all problems was to postpone any definite decision until the weather improved, or, failing that, until the next morning, or to the morning after, or to the morning after that. Art's philosophy was centred around the proposition that the weather ran the expedition, not him.

When he had helped Bruce unload the green canoe, Skip was at first puzzled to find so much water in the bottom, then angry when he discovered the hole. He launched into one of his best "Group Consideration and Altruistic Behavior" speeches, well punctuated with righteous indignation at us bowmen in general, and me in particular. Bruce was apologetic. Joe moved off. Having had more than my fill of Skip's altruism, I went on the attack.

"If you looked after your own damned business instead of minding everyone else's, you wouldn't have a hole in your God-damned canoe, and we would all be better off...."

Art, Pete, Joe and Bruce busied themselves elsewhere setting up camp.

The next morning, Skip patched the hole with "canoe glue." We shot the rapids without difficulty and arrived before evening at a lovely campsite. The morning after that, we took a holiday to kill our second caribou, then continued down the river and across another lake, then paddled down the river the following day until held up by the big gorge and bad weather for the next four days.

"SIX!... SEVEN!" Bruce shouted. Art dropped the serving spoon back into the pot, walked back to the rear entrance of the tarpaulin and sat down on a wet rock.

When Art had set up his tarp, he had placed the cooking fire on the leeward end so that the wind would blow through the tarp and carry the smoke away. He had placed two wooden boxes, one the dishes were stored in and a second which held the repair kit, under the tarp by the fire. These were the only two warm and dry seats in camp; and on previous occasions we bowmen had left them vacant for Art and Skip, in deference to their position as cooks and leaders, and to the fact that it was Art's tarp — but this morning, sitting next to Skip on Art's box was Bruce.

Earlier in the trip, while we were still on Black Lake, the sole of Bruce's boot had come unstitched. It would have been possible to have turned around then, to allow Bruce to buy another pair of boots at the Hudson's Bay store at Stony Rapids; but we had already been delayed by my late arrival, by the wrong cases of peanut butter in glass jars, by the forgotten canoe paddles, and by windy weather.

When Bruce had held up his right foot for all to see the flapping sole coming off his boot, I had had the sinking feeling that Art would turn back.

"Art?" Bruce had called out plaintively. "What do you think I should do about it?" He seemed to be pressuring Art to turn back to Stony Rapids. I watched Art anxiously, fearing he would oblige Bruce, and the expedition would end up cancelled.

We had been drifting then on a calm lake in the middle of the night. The sun was glowing pink beyond the northern horizon. Bruce, anticipating the slow amputation of frost-bitten toes by Art's dull hunting knife, continued to hold his foot in the air. Art hesitated.

We had drifted in the canoes for a long time before Art made up his mind. Finally he said: "Well, if I were you, Bruce, I would write Mr. L.L. Bean a letter: 'Dear Mr. Bean: You son-of-a-bitch. Love, Bruce'."

Art picked up his paddle and continued down the lake.

Everyone laughed but Bruce, who looked more dejected than ever.

"There's stuff in the repair kit, Bruce," Skip had said sympathetically. "You can have whatever you need to fix your boot."

The following day, Bruce showed off the repairs he had made. The look of concern for his foot had not disappeared. He had tried to hold the boot together with tape; later he was to make more durable repairs — but he was never to rely on Art again. It was to Skip that he turned for support thereafter.

[I wore Army boots. Everyone else on the trip followed Art's recommendation and wore boots from L.L. Bean. By the end of the trip, all our boots were in rough shape; but generally speaking, the L.L. Bean boots held up as well as the Army boots, and the Army buys strong boots. Art had worn L.L. Bean boots on all his trips and swore by them. They were made of soft moccasin leather, which was comfortable, light-weight, and strong. Bruce had just had bad luck.]

Two months later, as we waited by the gorge, Bruce had not forgotten Art's little joke at his foot's expense. He kept Art in his sights as Art filled his pannikin full of oatmeal.

Art dropped the serving spoon back into the nearly empty pot, poured some watered-down powdered milk over his soggy oatmeal, and stumbled over the rocks, oblivious to Bruce's hostility. Ducking his head, Art entered the tarp from the rear, sitting down on a wet rock.

He had just become settled when he mumbled something under his breath in the nature of an imprecation and crawled out from under the tarp to retrieve his can of sugar, which he had left back in his tent. After brushing through the wet willow bushes, he returned through the rain to the tarp and sat down once again on the wet rock. A gust of wind shook the tarp and sprayed cold water down his neck and into his oatmeal.

"From now on, this tarp is going to be divided into two parts: one for the cooks, and one for the *hoi poloi*," Art announced.

There was silence except for the flapping of the canvas and the squalls of rain pounding on it.

At the other end of the tarp sat Bruce, warmed by the fire, his back turned to Art. Bruce said something to Skip, who was sitting next to him on the other box by the fire, his back also turned towards Art. Skip whispered a reply to Bruce. Neither turned to reply to Art, and neither moved. They continued to eat their oatmeal in comfort.

I came around to the back of the tarp and sat by Art. "Not 'the' *hoi poloi*," I corrected, in a friendly way. "'*Hoi*' means 'the' in Greek, so the 'the' is redundant. Just *hoi poloi*."

"I stand corrected," Art mumbled and scooped another spoonful of cold, watery oatmeal into his mouth while water dripped down both our necks.

That evening, after dinner, Skip announced that we had nearly run out of powdered milk. He asked us if we would prefer to preserve the quantity by adding more water, or preserve the quality by cutting back on the quantity. Art spoke in favor of preserving the quality (such as it was), on the grounds that watering it down yet again just meant adding more cold water to our oatmeal and our tea.

Art's logic did not prevail. If in the beginning of the trip we had all automatically agreed with him, now we all automatically disagreed.

For the sake of democracy, Skip said he would honor the wishes of the majority; and so the wishes of Peter Franck and the United Bowmen's Association carried, and Art's objection was ignored, and Skip became *de facto* leader of the expedition.

The following evening, the rain had stopped, and there were signs of clearing in the west. Mumbling something about migrating geese upstream, Art picked up his camera and left the evening campfire. Peter and Skip went downstream to scout the gorge yet one more time.

When the sternmen were gone, we bowmen sat around the campfire roasting Art and the caribou meat. Although the weather had been wet, it had also been fairly warm, so the meat was now crawling with maggots. When roasted, the maggots tasted like fried eggs; but despite their delicious flavor, they gave off an aura of symbolic rottenness to the camp.

As darkness settled over the rapids, Skip returned. Bruce asked him to speak to Art about the amount of oatmeal he had been taking each morning. "He trusts you, Skip," he added with persuasive flattery.

Skip frowned, then looked around at each of us as if to ask if we agreed with Bruce. "Yes, he trusts

you, Skip," I said sardonically. Skip started to say
something, looked down at the ground, looked at Joe,
looked at me, hesitated, then nodded his head and
walked away.

The following morning, the wind was up and
Art still had not made a decision; but finally he
asserted his authority by telling us bowmen to portage
a load of indispensable equipment over the cliff. He
and the other sternmen would scout the gorge one
more time before shooting it with lightened canoes.

As we bowmen climbed to the top of the cliff and
descended the far side, the sky clouded over and rain
squalls showered us yet again for the third straight
day. Bruce and Joe decided to take shelter under a
ledge until the squalls passed, but I preferred to walk
back to camp alone. By the time I returned, I was
drenched.

Art and Skip emerged from their tents
noticeably dry. Art was very solicitous of my well
being, and volunteered to ring out my socks for me,
which I thought showed generosity of spirit above
and beyond the call of duty because they had not been
washed since the beginning of the trip except by
muskeg water squishing in and out of my increasingly
dilapidated boots and by the rain.

> August 15th: ... All along we could see
> it was a very heavy current and big
> waves. We were hungry. It was late now
> and I was tired. I knew this was no time
> to make a decision.

Three days later, Art had still not made a decision, and the United Bowmen's Association was preparing a *coup d'etat*; but on the following day, Art loaded his canoe and took Skip down the rapids as his bowman. Skip took Peter through as his bowman on the second run. Bruce approached me, asking if he could take my place in the third canoe. I asked him why. "For the thrill of it," he said. Bruce, the thrill-seeking sportsman, had emerged. I said, "Sure."

As it turned out, the portaging had been an unnecessary precaution: the rapids in the gorge were no worse than many others we had shot. But perhaps Art had been right to be cautious, even if we had wasted the better part of four days. In the wilderness, it is both easy and fatal to get careless; and after the gorge, Art did get careless.

> August 20th: Today we shot a couple of heavy but short rapids, only the second of which I looked over. Not very smart of me. I probably should be more careful.

We reloaded the canoes, and continued down the river to the verge of Dubawnt Lake, and camped that night on a lovely site.

"Skip says my pannikin is causing grumbling among the men since they think I'm getting more than they are," Art wrote in his diary. "Could be. Will use bowl from now on."

Much to everyone's surprise, when Art came down to breakfast the following morning, he left his aluminum pannikin in the pot box and picked up the sixth, beige, bakelite bowl which was identical to the ones the rest of us ate out of.

The weather was fine for paddling, but we had eaten the last of the second caribou; and so despite the fact that we had spent five of the previous seven days idle, and Autumn was upon us, we voted for the holiday because we were out of meat. Everyone voted for the holiday, that is, but Peter Franck. Bruce went to hunt, Peter to fish, Joe to pick blueberries, Skip to gather mushrooms, Art to take pictures, and I to wash my socks.

Mushrooms had sprouted up everywhere in great profusion: many varieties, of all shapes and colors. No one on the trip knew anything about mushrooms; but during our three days at the gorge, Skip had volunteered to test one of the more common types on himself. He had not dropped dead, so we presumed that one type was safe to eat.

Noble Skip. I had watched his experiment with more than culinary interest.

While Bruce was on the hunt and Art was following him around with his camera, I borrowed Art's axe to cut some wood to boil the water to wash my socks. I found a black spruce tree that seemed to be several hundred years old. It came up to my waist in height and was the only wood I found. It was also the last spruce tree we were to see. Tiny dwarf birch and willow were still to eke out a bonsai existence in the shelter of rocks and in valleys, but none grew more than knee high as we continued north.

One swing of the axe and I struck a rock. Most of the wood of the tree was buried in moss. I decided that washing my socks was not worth the life of this tree and spent the remainder of the day filing out the chink in Art's axe.

After many hours of filing, the chink was gone; but then again, so was about half an inch of Art's axe. The blade was very shiny and noticeably shorter. I put the axe back in its leather sheath and buried it deep in Art's pack, hoping he would not have occasion to use it until the blade weathered a bit.

Bruce returned from the hunt and led me back to the dead caribou. I skinned and butchered it. We carried the meat back to camp, and I handed the hide over to Skip, who had requested it. Skip accused me of doing a particularly terrible job of skinning the animal as further proof of my lack of "GROUP CONSIDERATION AND ALTRUISTIC BEHAVIOR."

Dinner was a splendid affair: delicious trout Peter had caught, the best cuts of meat from the caribou Bruce had shot, savory mushrooms of the variety Skip had tested at the previous gorge — all topped off with buckets of blueberries picked by Joe. The sun set over our beautiful campsite, lapped against by the clear waters of the fast Dubawnt River; and the land was elegant in autumnal dress under a colorful evening sky.

Across the river on a stony ridge, a delicate structure of rocks built by long dead Innuit hunters marked the entrance to Dubawnt Lake. We had passed out of Chipewyan country through "no man's land" into Innuit country; but the Innuit were long since gone, and the rocks were silent.

After dinner, Art asked who had borrowed his axe. I confessed. Much to my surprise, instead of criticizing me for borrowing it without permission, he bathed me in gratitude. During his six trips into the wilderness, he said, everyone had borrowed his axe: but I was the first person who had ever sharpened it for him. I was very happy to have done something that pleased Art for a change; but the following day, as we entered Dubawnt Lake, there would be no more trees to cut — and his axe would never be used again.

photo credit Sports Illustrated
Skip Pessl

138

Chapter Fifteen
His Hour Come Round At Last

Skip was furious. He was so angry he slammed the bow of his green canoe full speed onto the rocky bank. Jumping out of his seat, he scrambled forward over the load, looking as if he were going to kill Art. Fortunately, he lost his balance and ended up in the water with the contents of his capsized canoe on top of him.

It had been a marvellous day. An unusual sunny, south wind had been blowing, and giant waves had been sweeping us towards the end of Dubawnt Lake. Dubawnt Lake is a large lake, about fifty miles across and a hundred miles in extent. Because of its size, the waves tended to be large. We could see one another when all three canoes were on the crest of a wave, but not when any one was in a trough; there was a rhythm to our connectedness, yet by noon the rhythm had become more and more attenuated.

After a while, Skip and Bruce in the green canoe, and Peter and I in the red canoe, realized that we had not seen the grey canoe for a long time. We pulled alongside one another and searched the horizon for some sign of Art and Joe. We saw a flashing light in the distance, which we guessed was the sun reflecting off Joe's paddle as he drove the grey canoe over the crests of waves towards an island. By silently counting the flashes, we surmised that he was paddling fast. We feared the grey canoe had taken on water. Because they were too far away for us to be of any immediate assistance, we just drifted and watched.

When finally we saw them reach the island and disappear around the lee side, we breathed a sigh of relief; but then Skip and I fell (not surprisingly) into an argument. He wanted to turn our canoes broadside to the waves and go check on Art and Joe to make sure they were safe. I felt that he was, as usual, being unnecessarily paternalistic. I favored continuing on in the direction of wind and waves and to let Art and Joe catch up to us when and if they desired.

Bruce and Pete kept out of the argument; and for a long time we drifted down the lake, hoping the grey canoe would reappear around the far side of the island and thereby settle the argument, but it never did reappear, and so finally Skip picked up his paddle and swung his green canoe around. Pete turned our red canoe to accompany him, and after more than an hour of struggling broadside to the now dangerous waves, we neared the island. From a cliff we heard Art's voice yell down to us. "Hold it guys, I want to get you coming in on a big one." The next wave nearly swamped our canoes. We heard Art's camera "whirr," and then he said, "O.K. Got it!"

Skip's face turned various shades of crimson: his grip tightened on his paddle. Rounding the cliff to the safety of a calm cove, he drove the bow of his canoe up a flat rock, sprang out of his seat, and managed to lose his footing and tip his canoe over on top of himself.

Skip and Art had very different modes of leadership, which stemmed from different objectives. From the beginning of the trip, Skip had seen the Barren Grounds as something to be conquered, like Mount Everest, as quickly as possible. To cross them safely, he believed we would all have to sacrifice our individual "interests, appetites and passions" for the good of the expedition. Skip believed it was his duty, as second-in-command, first to set a noble example, second to support Art, and third to reprove those of us who fell short of his high standards. His willingness to stand last in line for food, to wash dishes as well as to cook breakfast, and to always act in an upright manner, resulted in everyone having the highest respect for him. It was to Skip that even I turned when we needed some delicacy, like fish roe, divided up equally. He was always fair, and he always reserved the last and least portion for himself; but, as Mark Twain once observed, "Nothing is quite so difficult to live with as the annoyance of someone else's good example."

Skip was very noble, but he lacked inner peace. As the trip progressed, everyone but Skip had become tolerant of each other's foibles. We had accepted that Art did not like to kill animals, but that Bruce was a sportsman who did; and we had come to understand both sentiments.

We accepted that Joe liked his creature comforts, and also accepted that Skip liked to both cook breakfast and wash dishes. Joe may not have been as noble as Skip, but he was less self-righteous and had a better sense of humor; each had his merits and we accepted both, but if we were becoming more and more tolerant of one another, Skip was becoming more and more intolerant of us. Towards the end of August, his anger flared out not just at me, but also at the others with increasing frequency: and on the day of the big waves, his rage exploded at Art.

For Art, the wilderness was not a hostile but a Holy place. We were not on an expedition to "conquer" the Barrens, and therefore Art did not feel the need to run the expedition like an Army on an assault. Art's spiritual destination was inner peace. Arrival at this inner destination takes time, and so Art took his time and sipped his tea, and turned the running of the expedition over to the weather.

There is a Buddhist joke about a pilgrim seeking enlightenment. He asks his master how long it will take. The master replies: "Ten years."

The pilgrim protests: "No! No! What if I work really hard?"

"Twenty years," the master replies.

Holy men send their pilgrims towards a physical destination at first because, before enlightenment, the pilgrim needs faith in a tangible objective; but if a pilgrim walks slowly enough, the seven deadly sins fall away, and the Garden of Eden is discovered within him or herself. When one has reached that destination, other destinations seem trivial, even while falling off a cliff.

During the course of the trip, Art had never hurried. He gave us time to make our own pilgrimage; and by the time we had rebelled three times against his leadership, he had tacitly stepped aside to enjoy his tea in peace. Art had not formally resigned, but we bowmen had rejected so many of his recent decisions (about rationing the sugar, mixing the powdered milk, paddling before or after breakfast) that he was *de facto* no longer in charge. Art had accepted our rejection with equanimity and now ate out of the same bowls as the rest of us to symbolize his acceptance of equality; but for Skip, the situation was more ambiguous.

In the movie "The Emerald Forest," an American engineer meets a native chief in the jungles of Brazil. Members of the tribe have captured the engineer's son. The engineer tells the chief to order his tribe to release his son. The chief says. "If I tried to tell them what to do, I would no longer be chief."
When Art stepped aside as leader and picked up the same size bowl as the rest of us, he ceased to be leader in the outward hierarchical sense, but became once again our leader in the inward spiritual sense.
Rebellion is a substitute for inner peace. It gives meaning and purpose to life so long as the object of

the rebellion remains in power, because that object is seen as the cause of one's discontent: but once the authority disintegrates, it becomes necessary to seek more deeply — and as we searched more deeply, we discovered that the source of our inner discontent was not Art, but our own gluttony, our own sloth, our own anger, our own lust, our own avarice, our own envy, our own vanity. Particularly our vanity; and so when we looked over to Art sipping his tea in that peaceful, meditative way of his, we too began to reach for the tea pot and to emulate him once again.

If the weather was unfavorable for paddling, or the waves were too big, or the auguries were unpropitious, or a holiday was called for to celebrate the return of good weather, or at any rate, if life was too good to hurry, Art would pour himself another cup of tea, and now so did we.

Somewhere on our pilgrimage, we had lost our desire to exchange the Garden of Eden for the rat race of civilization. Holidays became no longer occasions for anxiety attacks, but an opportunity to appreciate the peace within and the beauty without. So while rebelling against Art in some respects, we had begun to emulate him more deeply in others; we too celebrated each holiday as if it were a Holy Day bathed in grace, fed by the caribou, washed by the rain and warmed by the sun, while Peter climbed the walls of his tent and Skip exploded in anger.

Skip had been into the wilderness twice before with Art, and had seen himself as Art's most devoted disciple; but what Art seemed to be asking now was for us to accompany him over the edge of the Abyss.

Skip hesitated. He was not quite ready for that reality.

There is a Buddhist joke about a disciple seeking enlightenment. For years, the disciple pesters the master to teach him. Eventually the master pushes the disciple off a cliff. Remembering himself as a teacher of wisdom, he yells to the falling disciple: "You'll find enlightenment on the way down."

Boxed into a corner, Skip could do little more than scowl at our decisions, whether he liked them or not, especially if Peter was preoccupied elsewhere, buried in his gear trying to pack up the expedition single-handedly. Earlier in the trip Skip had abstained from expressing his opinions as part of his contribution to "Group Consideration and Altruistic Behavior," and so we had fallen out of the habit of consulting him. As a result, the expedition did not move far in those last pleasant weeks of August.

Each morning we would wait for Peter Franck to leave the breakfast fire to pack his things. We bowmen and Art would discuss the schedule of the day. We already knew what Peter's vote would be, so we felt no need to consult him. After we bowmen had finished our discussion, we informed rather than consulted Skip. Outwardly, Skip said nothing; but inwardly, he grew more angry by the day.

Skip had done all the right things during the course of the trip, but now we bowmen had decided that wisdom did not lie so much in conquest as in surrender. Peter stammered protests, and Skip frowned; but we bowmen ruled. While Summer passed into Autumn, and Autumn into Winter without us getting any nearer to the outpost at Baker Lake, Skip found himself in the difficult position of having become second-in-command to a cup of tea. He seemed to have desired a more civilized schedule, something along the lines of shift work at General Motors where his father held an important executive position; but Art only smiled sweetly and sipped his tea.

One day, Art pulled into an island to cook lunch. We were running out of hard tack and other luncheon supplies; so instead of a cold lunch, Art decided to boil up a pot of fish soup, the fish having been caught by Skip that morning. Uncharacteristically, Skip went for a walk and did not return until we were through eating. Because for so long he had always stood last in line, we decided to save an extra-large portion of this specially delicious soup for Skip in Art's pannikin, the old symbol of leadership. We were very happy with our own generosity, and reflected warmly on how proud Skip would be of us for at last following his example of self-sacrifice when we handed him this extra-large ration. But when he returned and examined the contents of Art's pannikin, instead of being overwhelmed with gratitude, Skip exploded in rage and accused us of cheating him as we had always been cheating him throughout the trip. We hung our heads in embarrassment, and Skip ate his fish soup in silence.

Skip had frequently expressed anger at Joe and me, occasionally at Bruce, but never openly at Art. But now, after that day of high waves, as he scrambled over the load in the green canoe from his stern seat, Skip appeared to want to kill Art. We all stood around watching, wondering what would happen, but some pagan god intervened and cooled Skip's temper by dumping him in the water. When Skip extricated himself from his over-turned canoe, and crawled onto shore dripping wet, he looked ridiculous, and everyone was trying not to laugh.

For a long time Skip, water dripping off his sodden clothes, stood before Art: our two dauntless leaders. We all waited silently. Then, after a while, Skip seemed to have understood the joke: we were where we wanted to be, that heavenly place of inner peace. We no longer needed a leader to get us there, and there was no need to hurry. Skip smiled and Art smiled back, and then we all laughed except Peter Franck. I picked up my .22 and went to shoot a ptarmigan I had spotted.

On the edge of the Abyss, there are no leaders, only penguins standing around waiting to see who would be the first to jump into the jaws of death where the sea lions wait.

The following day, Art announced that Skip would continue cooking breakfast, but Skip would not be washing any more dishes; and after that Skip voted with us for yet another Holy Day, and another, and another, and everyone was perfectly happy except Peter Franck.

photo credit George Luste
An Innuit Cairn overlooking the Dubawnt River.

Chapter Sixteen
I Was the River

The lake had been flat calm and mirrored the sky out to the horizon where the two joined in oblivion. All day we had paddled towards that distant horizon, but the faster we paddled the faster it receded. For many weeks we had paddled towards it, but we never reached it. Behind us was the same scene, sky and lake meeting together on the edge of oblivion. At first I had felt bored; my boredom turned to anxiety; then to panic.

On the Barrens, nothing had a name. There were no street signs, no people, no spoken words: we had been surrounded for more than forty days by nothing but "miles and miles of nothing but miles and miles." This time, when I panicked, I had the feeling, as in a nightmare, that I was paddling and paddling, trying to escape some undefined danger; but no matter how hard I paddled, I could not escape my fate.

I propped a book up in the bow and tried to read. Earlier in the trip, I had been interested in the book, the Penguin edition of William James's *Psychology*; but now it seemed meaningless and irrelevant.

William James had had a nervous breakdown while studying in Germany, but I was having my own nervous breakdown and could not get interested in his. As the day wore on, I drifted in and out of consciousness, nearly asleep at the paddle.

Suddenly I awoke and slammed my paddle handle across the gunwales and held on to the canoe with all my strength. I had had the feeling that the lake was swallowing me alive. I looked down at the water. The canoe was still afloat. The bow sliced quietly through the flat calm. Whirlpools from my paddle spun themselves out. Behind as in front of the canoe, the lake was mirror-flat out to the horizon, as if we had never passed over it. That was it! I had ceased to exist! I had never existed! It was all a dream!

Reality and dream seemed interchangeable, and both were nightmares. My name, my identity as a human being, was spinning itself out like the whirlpools from my paddle and disappearing into the endless nothingness of the flat calm lake.

This panic attack was different from the earlier one. Then, I had been afraid of breaking a leg, starving, freezing — in short, afraid of tangible physical dangers. This time, I feared that my soul had been vaporized by the wilderness.

I could remember my past life, but only as if it were a bad movie I had dreamed about. Was the former-me the person who had lived in the nightmare and the new-me the person who had awakened into reality, or was the former-me the real person and the now-lost-in-the-wilderness-me living the nightmare?

The philosopher Alfred North Whitehead talks of "process" and "being." The "process" is the food chain, where everything passes into everything else. But there is also "being," which revolts against the nothingness of death and struggles to assert its individual identity. In civilization, we run the rat race to establish our identity, to put a portrait of ourselves on the wall, to die with a big tombstone over our corpse: but in the wilderness, who knows the name of that caribou which had died for us? In the wilderness, universals live for ever: but individuals are born, eat, and die without a name, without a soul. The further we travelled into the wilderness, the more my soul seemed to be disintegrating into caribou meat.

When we had first met the caribou, I had felt so grateful to it that I had wanted it to become one with me, and I one with it, not just physically by eating it, but spiritually by making a religious ritual of its death and resurrection through me. I had been more than willing to surrender my old civilized soul for a caribou steak, but now I was beginning to understand the other half of the equation. Eating caribou steak was one thing, abandoning my civilized identity to become nothing more than 156 pounds of caribou meat along the food chain was another.

I was no longer even 156 pounds of meat; after forty days of fasting in the wilderness, I was mostly skin and bones. Joining the food chain to bring my weight back up to its civilized level was reasonable enough in my eyes, provided I was the animal doing the eating, and not vice versa; but having my soul

measured by the criterion of a butcher shop had
suddenly made me nervous. What voyage of spiritual
oblivion had Art embarked us upon anyway?

Looking back on my previous life, I could not
remember doing anything worth remembering except
carrying on the name of my ancestors, and I had never
been very good at that; but I had no other identity.

My mother's ancestors had been less
"distinguished" than my father's. She laid claim to
Commodore Preble, who had been a merchant sea
captain sailing out of Portland, Maine. During the
war of 1812, Congress had decided that America
needed an official Navy, instead of a bunch of pirates
like the Revolutionary captain, John Paul Jones.
After dumping the first eight "Commodores" for
cowardice, Congress hired my mother's great, great,
great uncle, "Old Pepper;" but generally speaking,
my mother's side of the family were artisans and
farmers, rather than wealthy political crooks with
expensive portraits of themselves on the wall.

To the left of the fireplace in our library, there
was a portrait of one of my father's great
grandfathers, Nathaniel Tracy, painted by John
Trumbull. To the right, another great grandfather,
Thomas Amory, painted by Stuart. According to my
father's tradition, Nathaniel Tracy had been the
richest man in America at the time of the War for
Independence; but my mother had always referred
to him as "frog legs" because of his tight yellow pants.
She claimed he had made his fortune by carrying
slaves from Africa to the Southern States and by

running rum up from the Caribbean. She could always find something disparaging to say about my father's side of the family.

My father's mother's mother had been a "Lee," and in my grandmother's living room were two full-length portraits of General Lee and his wife by Copley, reaching from the floor to the ceiling. My mother was quick to point out that this "General Lee" was not the famous "General Lee" from Virginia who had led the Confederate Army, but the Revolutionary General Lee who had been court-martialled by General George Washington for fleeing in a cowardly manner from the British at the Battle of Monmouth.

The competition over ancestors in my family ran deep. My father's father had paid a genealogist a minor furtune to trace his ancestors back through six kings of England and eight kings of France to the Emperor Charlemagne, crowned in 800 A.D. From my mother's point of view, this was like tracing one's ancestors back to Attila the Hun.

In contrast, my mother's favorite ancestor was her bachelor uncle, Fred Rolfe, a school teacher who had bought a homestead on the shore of Indian Pond in the backwoods of New Hampshire. He left it to her when he died; and instead of taking us to Southampton, Long Island to live in wealth and splendor in the summer home of my father's mother, my mother retreated with us to this homestead to grow our own food. There was no running water, no electricity, no refrigeration. Every morning at dawn, my mother walked five miles to pick up the day's milk from the nearest farmer, Fay Emory, who still ploughed his fields with oxen, still cut his hay with a scythe, still pitched it into the hay loft with a fork, and still milked his two cows by hand. On our homestead, we hand-pumped our water from a well, read at night by kerosene lanterns, used an outhouse, and made a lot of cottage cheese out of all that sour milk.

My mother's grandfather had been a cooper. He had made barrels in Portland, Maine. Her father had won a scholarship to Harvard, and had become a Harvard Professor of Economics, and that is how my mother met my father: he as a student at Harvard, and she as the daughter of a Professor, but they came from different worlds.

I liked my father more than my mother; he was more gentle, more peaceful, and more kind. *The Wall Street Journal* had referred to him as the "genius of Wall Street," not because he had made a "killing" on the Stock Market (he hadn't), but because he had proposed a law which would regulate investment banking in such a way that it would benefit society as a whole, instead of just the rich. He believed that an investment banker should be like a patron of the Arts who supported beautiful enterprises, not a pirate who bought, sold, and liquidated corporations for quick personal profit. Not surprisingly, his proposed legislation was never passed into law.

Although I loved my father and his futile quest to bring love, justice and truth to Wall Street, I was more attracted to the American way of life represented by mother's side of the family. After my father's death and after despairing of a relationship with my jet-setting Zaidee, I had repaired to that old homestead in the backwoods of New Hampshire to lick my wounds and boil up ground hogs for dinner; then to the Army, and now to the Arctic, in search of my own truth, beauty and identity.

I loved the spiritual purity of the Arctic wilderness; I felt I had come to the source of all truth, beauty and life. But when I discovered that my only identity in the wilderness was as meat on the food chain like a ground hog, I became more than nervous; I collapsed into yet another "spiritual crisis."

During the course of the trip, my feelings for the wilderness had waxed and waned. In the first few weeks, I had been so eager to escape the catastrophe of my civilized identity that I had hurled my coins joyfully into the lake; but by the time the expedition had reached the Height of Land, I wished I had never been so foolish. I wanted to turn around, recover my coins, live near a hospital, fill my belly with civilized food, and inherit the wealth of my ancestors, even if they had been crooks.

As the days went by, I did not break a leg or get an appendicitis, and so I stopped worrying for a while. After forty days, when Art had asked us if we wanted to turn back, I was eager to continue on: and when we met the herds of caribou, I had embraced them body and soul; but now, four days later, I dreamed the wilderness was swallowing me alive.

In time, all things pass, including my second panic attack. The night we killed our second caribou, the pendulum had swung back. I dreamed that the sky was my new mother and the land my new father. I imagined myself to be the river, cradled by the land and nourished by the sky, all flowing together in peaceful harmony: and I fell into a deep and peaceful sleep.

Over the ensuing weeks, as we killed our third, fourth and fifth caribou, I came to experience civilization as more and more distant, more and more unattainable, more and more undesirable. Instead of taking my identity from civilization, I nurtured and caressed the vision of me as the river, fed by mother sky and father earth, until I felt more at home in the wilderness than I had ever felt in civilization.

In time, my dream world of mother sky and father earth ceased feeling like a dream and felt more like reality, while my former civilized world seemed increasingly unreal, more like a bad dream from which I was glad to have been awakened and to which I no longer wished to return.

"So you lost your sense of reality," the young RCMP officer had said.

It had not seemed like a loss to me at the time. The reality I had discovered was the reality of the Garden of Eden, the most beautiful reality I have ever experienced.

On the day Skip Pessl was drying his clothes after he had fallen into the lake, I went to hunt ptarmigan. I killed five with my .22 before running out of ammunition, then killed two more with my hunting knife.

Ptarmigan are Arctic grouse and are notoriously easy to kill. I threw my knife at one of the ptarmigan, and the blade went right through its heart — which surprised me, even if ptarmigan are easy to kill.

I am reasonably good with a knife, but not that good. What surprised me even more was that when I threw my knife at the seventh ptarmigan, which had already taken flight, my blade found its way to its heart as well. Bird and blade fell to the ground together in an embrace of death.

I had heard of *Zen and the Art of Archery*, but I had not realized I had achieved such a close relationship with that which I was trying to eat.

There is usually a sense of guilt about killing anything, but my hunger was more real to me than guilt. By the end of the second month in the wilderness, the portraits of my ancestors on the wall meant nothing to me. I accepted that I was part of the food chain, and that was all that I was: so I did not have to feel guilty about killing a ptarmigan. The ptarmigan would become part of me, and I of it, body and soul for a time, until we both passed into the Universal Beauty of the Wilderness.

A week before killing the ptarmigan with my hunting knife, I had left the campfire to go back to the tent Peter and I shared. I had felt sick from eating mushrooms. They had not been poisonous. There are no poisonous mushrooms in the Arctic, I had just eaten too many of them. We had recently killed our third caribou and it was hanging on a tripod by the lake, where the wind would keep the blow flies from laying their maggot eggs. A wolf had spotted the meat and was walking down the gully where Peter had pitched our tent out of the wind. As I rounded the corner of the cliff, I ran into the wolf. It dropped into position to spring at my throat. I held out my hand to offer the nice doggy something to eat. It stared at me, and I stared at it. After a while, it backed off dragging its forelegs along the moss so as to be able to defend itself if I followed. When a safe distance away, it turned and trotted off, then turned back and, like that psychiatrist who had purchased our house in New York City, took a second look at me as if to analyze my particular brand of insanity.

Because we had lost the sensation of getting anywhere, we began to spend more and more time hunting, fishing and gathering berries. The more time we spent hunting, fishing and gathering wilderness fruit, the more at home we felt on the tundra; but although life was very pleasant, and we took more and more holidays, feelings of anxiety still welled up within me from time to time. One day, I picked up a pretty stone on the beach and watched the waves curl and break and then rejoin the water. The wave was more beautiful than the stone, but part of me still wanted my name to endure longer than the time it takes for a wave to break on the shore. I put the pretty pebble in my pocket, like a tombstone to endure with me forever as a symbol of my eternal soul.

Later in the trip, on September 12th, two days before Art was to die, when I believed that I too was going to die before finding a wife, I climbed a quartzite mountain and watched the sun setting over the colorful wilderness. In a land where beauty abounds, this spot out-did itself. On top of this miniature mountain, there was an alpine meadow; and on a ledge near that meadow a grave, a pile of rocks where some ancient Innuit hunter had been buried. There was no headstone giving his name, just the growing darkness. I felt close to him as if he were my spiritual ancestor, more so even than the portraits of my ancestral pirates painted on the walls at home; but then some inner urge towards immortality surfaced yet again. I stamped my foot and yelled out to the wilderness in defiance of its anonymous vastness: "I name this place 'Grinnell Mountain'."

The air carried my words away like the whirlpools from my paddle on the lake we had passed over weeks earlier, and all was stillness once again in the growing darkness.

I looked uneasily around to see if any of the others had chanced to climb this mountain behind me and had witnessed my vanity. I saw nothing but the beauty of the sun setting over a land frozen in purples, diamonds and gold.

photo credit George Luste
The barren ground.

Chapter Seventeen
On His Own

C-C-Crazy, he stammered." "Everyone has g-g-gone crazy."

Peter Franck was sitting cross-legged on his air mattress, his head making a bulge in the side of our "A-frame" mountain tent. "One d-d-day, everyone panics; we get up before d-d-dawn and k-k-kill ourselves paddling all d-d-day, and the next d-d-day we take a holiday, and then another, and then another. It m-m-makes no s-s-sense! I mean I love it here. I want to come b-b-back; but this is m-m-madness! Everyone has gone c-c-crazy...."

Peter Franck had never spoken before, except in brief sentences; but now an irrepressible torrent of words came flooding forth. He seemed very distraught. I lay on my air mattress propped up by my elbow and nodded my head as I had seen my psychiatrist do.

"...m-m- madness. Everyone's g-g-gone insane...."

The date was August 29th; that day we had all voted (except Peter Franck, of course) to take yet another holiday, even though the weather was excellent for paddling. The official reason for the holiday was to celebrate reaching the end of Dubawnt Lake.

Actually, we had not reached the end of Dubawnt Lake, but we had almost reached the end; and our campsite, like so many of our previous campsites during the last weeks of August, had a splendid view of the surrounding countryside; and so we did that day as we had done on those previous days, we voted to take another holiday. It had seemed like a perfectly rational thing to do from our point of view; but in Peter's eyes, taking all those holidays was insane.

"... c-c-crazy...."

In the last two months, we had fallen about a month behind schedule. Winter storms would be waiting for us in a couple of days, to say nothing of Peter's not being able to get back to Harvard in time for registration. In his eyes, our celebrations were more than premature; they were sheer lunacy.

"It's nothing but m-m-madness!" he repeated. "I mean Art's a g-g-great g-g-guy, but I c-c-can't stand it any more. Everyone has gone c-c-crazy...."

While I, and my fellow bowmen, had gyrated through emotional turmoil, loving and fearing the wilderness, voting for holidays, voting against holidays, Peter Franck had always remained steady. He had kept track of how far we had gone and how far we had yet to go in order to reach the outpost at Baker Lake by September 2nd, and the figures did not add up.

Because Peter had planned to enter his sophomore year at Harvard that Autumn, the

September 2nd date was particularly important to him. He would have to travel to Cambridge, Massachusetts and register for classes within a few days of our return. He had pointed this out to Art and to the rest of us several times in the early days of the trip, when it first became apparent that we were falling behind schedule; but no one had taken his concerns very seriously.

Joe and Bruce, who were also entering their sophomore years (at Dartmouth), told him not to worry, there was always late registration; but Pete had continued to worry — and, as we fell further and further behind, he worried more and more. While the rest of us went on laughing at Art's little ironies like "We've got all summer," Peter began to get serious and save bits of hardtack in empty peanut butter jars.

"... m-m-madness...."

"Yes..., yes..., yes...," (nod, nod).

The more he studied the calendar, and the more he checked our food supplies, the more worried he had become. In addition to protesting all holidays and storing away bits of food, he took to packing up earlier in the morning than anyone else, to loading our canoe before Art had finished sipping his breakfast tea, and to waiting in it for an hour or two, hoping Art would get the hint. Art had said nothing and had done nothing, except to go for leisurely bird walks and leave Peter to sit there in a state of elevated agitation.

"... c-c-crazy...."

"Yes..., yes..., yes...," (nod, nod).

Like Peter, I had had episodes of panic; but I had hid my fear from the others better than he. Showing fear, no matter how much a man may be feeling it, puts one at risk of being demoted to the bottom of the male hierarchy; it is therefore the first moral law of male masochism that no other male should ever be allowed to discover just how scared one really is.

"... insane...."

"Yes..., yes..., yes...," (nod, nod).

During my episodes of panic, I had found Peter's perpetual state of agitation reassuring. His concerns about our safety were so much deeper than mine, that I had begun to relax. I could not believe our situation to be as dangerous as he was constantly implying, and so his agitation helped me to put a brave face on things; but now he seemed so distressed that I began to fear he was in danger of going off the deep end, and so I nodded my head and said "Yes..., yes..., yes...," as I had seen my psychiatrist do.

"...c-c-crazy...."

"Yes..., yes..., yes...," (nod, nod).

By the time we bowmen had lost our fear of the wilderness and had taken effective control of the expedition, we had found it convenient to wait for Peter to go pack his things before discussing our plans for the day. We had learned long since how Peter felt about holidays, and therefore avoided arguments by not consulting him.

By the last week in August our plans, about which he had not been consulted, had consisted of taking time out for hunting, fishing, berry picking, relaxing, and exploratory side trips in the wrong direction. By August 31st, Peter was not only feeling isolated and ignored, but also paranoid, as if his concerns were being deliberately disregarded — which they were.

"...m-m-madness...."

"Yes..., yes..., yes...," (nod, nod).

I had learned how to play "psychiatrist" at Groton. Instead of tossing me down the dust chute in the old-fashioned way, the school had modernized its disciplinary system and had sent me to a psychiatrist instead. Although the dust chute probably would have proved more efficacious, I had learned a great deal from the psychiatrist. In particular, I had learned how to nod my head and reply "yes..., yes..., yes...." to anything and everything that was being said, just like Bruce LeFavour.

"...c-c-crazy...."

"Yes..., yes..., yes...," (nod, nod).

To make matters worse for him, Peter had me for a tent mate, and I was more crazy than the rest; I had not followed Art back into the Garden of Eden reluctantly, but enthusiastically. I had become Art's most devoted disciple. In addition to voting for holidays and pitching our tent in the most exposed locations, my attitude in the rapids had become cavalier, almost suicidal. Sometimes, as Peter and I approached a rapids, and the speed of the current quickened, I would lie back on the load rocked peacefully by the turbulent water, like a baby being cuddled in its mother's arms. This tended to cause Peter's nervous shiftings to increase by several orders of magnitude and the splashing from his paddle to come my way with ever-increasing intensity, until I sat up to avoid further drenching.

"...n-n-nuts...."

"Yes..., yes..., yes...," (nod, nod).

When we had met the caribou, the immediate threat of death by starvation had temporarily passed for the rest of us, and we had relaxed; but Peter had still voted against holidays and had continued to urge, in subtle and in not so subtle ways, that we keep our eyes on our professed objective to get across the Barrens before freeze-up.

"I c-c-can't understand what has g-g-gotten into everybody. We are s-s-supposed to be at B-B-Baker Lake in t-t-two more d-d-days, and we are only a little more than half way th-th-there, and we j-j-just took another h-h-holiday! It's c-c-crazy!"

We each thought the other had gone crazy, and to a certain extent we each had, in that we were now living in different realities; but our feelings did not differ as much as it might appear on the surface.

A couple of nights prior to Peter's nocturnal outburst, I had dreamed that I had come across Art taking pictures of a stone bird in a valley. I had feared in the dream that the walls of an overhanging cliff were about to fall on top of him. I wanted to warn Art, but I felt that if I yelled out, the vibrations from my voice would cause the cliff to collapse: so I stood watching him in helpless silence.

Of course I never spoke of my dream, nor revealed to Peter or to any one else my inner anxieties about the impending disaster which Art and the rest of us were so obviously courting.

"...c-c-crazy..."

"Yes..., yes..., yes...," (nod, nod).

During one of our innumerable holidays a few days earlier, we bowmen had been sitting around the campfire chewing the fat off a recently killed caribou, and Peter had dropped by for a cup of tea. Joe Lanouette, who was almost equal to Bruce LeFavour in the brilliance of his social graces, had launched the absorbing and stimulating question: Which would we choose if our wish could be granted — the meal of our dreams that evening, or the woman of our dreams?

The answer had been so obvious that we all began describing our favorite deserts, saving the entrées and appetizers for later, but Peter looked at us in a puzzled fashion; and when Joe finally turned to him to bring him into the conversation, Peter said it was of a woman that he had been dreaming. We looked at him in disbelief, but he was serious.

On the surface, Peter's objective was to get back to Harvard; but beneath the surface there is some circumstantial evidence that it was not just the Harvard library he was eager to lose himself in. He never mentioned the name of any girl friend, but then he never mentioned anything else about his life either. Peter was a very private person.

During the holiday on the 29th of August, Art, Skip, Bruce and Joe built a cairn, Innuit style, placing a note in it to commemorate our achievement of

167

reaching (or almost reaching) the end of Dubawnt Lake. I had climbed a miniature mountain in the opposite direction and had contemplated the meaning of life.

In my cycle of insanity, that morning my desire to return to civilization had all but totally disappeared, and I was thinking about deserting the expedition to remain alone on Dubawnt Lake. I knew I would not last long, but death in this beautiful paradise had seemed preferable to life in the seven deadly sins of civilization; or at least that is how I represented my feelings to myself in the morning. By afternoon, romantic suicide had had less and less appeal; I had sunk into deeper depths of despondency Wallowing around in suicidal self-pity, I had observed a mosquito land on the back of my hand. The movements of the mosquito were groggy and slow because the temperature was around the freezing mark; she was an easy target, a sure kill. I had raised my hand, but hesitated.

There is an old Buddhist joke about a pilgrim who visited all the universities around the world, searching for the meaning of life. None of the professors' answers seemed satisfactory to him, and so he kept searching until he ended up at the mouth of a cave in the Himalayas where a bodhisatva resided. Everyone had assured the pilgrim that this Bodhisatva was the wisest man on Earth. If no other person could satisfy his quest, this Bodhisatva surely would. Trembling with anticipation after a lifetime of research, the pilgrim asked: "What is the meaning of life?"

"Life is like a fountain," the Bodhisatva replied.

"It is?" the pilgrim questioned sceptically.

"Isn't it?" asked the Bodhisatva.

Earlier in the trip, I had received so many mosquito bites that my arms had swollen up; but after the swelling subsided, I had become more or less immune to them. I watched the groggy mosquito stagger around in the cold trying to find a tender entry point.

I studied her actions. She seemed to know, if not the meaning of life, at least what she wanted to do to me; but I, like the Bodhisatva, had fallen into the spiritual abyss of unknowing. Suddenly the meaning of life came to me, as well as to the mosquito. If I were going to commit suicide, why not donate my blood?

I had lost my civilized sense of lust, but now I was filled with the desire to procreate the planet. I needed a mate. I wanted to raise children. I suddenly realized that what this planet needed in addition to five or six billion more mosquitoes was five or six billion more Grinnells; this was clearly the meaning of life. No wonder the Bodhisatva in his cave was at a loss when presented with the key question. He had failed to share his cave with a woman!

Enlightenment (of a sort) had at last come to me. Women are the vessels of the logos through which the blood of the food chain must flow. Oh wonderful Mother Earth who gives birth to us all!

Who needs lust when inspired by such an insight into the nature of womankind? I helped the mosquito into flight, and walked happily down the mountain.

There was, however, a problem. We had not seen any women in the wilderness, nor anyone else for that matter, and were not likely to see anyone until we arrived at the outpost at Baker Lake. There are no women living on the tundra these days, just stone cairns. All the native women hang around the cash registers in the Hudson's Bay Posts.

"I've g-g-got to g-g-get out of here. I c-c-can't stand it any more," Peter said, his entire body shaking with emotion.

What had enabled Peter to remain focused on returning to Harvard while the rest of us ventured off with Art into the spiritual Garden of Paradise is anyone's guess, but the vision of a woman can do wonderful things to a man.

"Yes..., yes..., yes...," (nod, nod).

Peter was in a difficult position. Because we shared a canoe and a tent, leaving the expedition to get back to his woman was awkward for him unless I agreed to go with him.

Aristotle says there are five logical ways to persuade your companion. If induction does not work, nor deduction, nor syllogisms, then one must resort to the fifth mode of logic, which is to keep talking.

"Art's a g-g-great g-g-guy. I l-l-love the Arctic; I want to c-c-come back, b-b-but I've got to g-g-get out of here...."

"O.K., I'll go with you."

"Everyone's gone n-n-nuts…. We t-t-took a holiday today, one t-t-two days ago, and another the d-d-day before that…!"

"I'll go with you."

"…c-c-crazy. Everyone has gone n-n-nuts…."

"Tomorrow, if you want to pack up and leave ahead of the others, it's O.K. with me."

"… madness. It doesn't make any sense. I mean I love it here. I want to c-c-come back. Art's a great g-g-guy, but everyone has gone c-c-crazy…"

Peter and I had always been the first over the portages and ours was the fastest canoe. I thought it might be fun to strike out on our own. We would make good time.

"If you want to leave, we'll leave."

"…insane…."

"If you want, I'll come with you." I repeated. "We'll pack up in the morning and take off. To hell with them."

"What?" he asked.

"I said, 'To hell with them'."

Peter stared at me as if he were trying to figure out if I were teasing him yet one more time.

"We've got most of the food in our canoe," I pointed out. "When they get hungry, they'll try their hardest to catch up to us."

Peter continued to stare at me. Lost in visions of Harvard or the Nirvana of a Radcliffe co-ed, he sat silently for a long time, then lay down and fell into a deep sleep.

The next morning, Peter and I got up, joined the others for breakfast, packed our canoe, and without saying another word, embarked down the lake.

Peter had his own set of maps which he secured in front of him by the straps of a canoe pack as he had seen Art do. At first I could feel the power of his paddle strokes, and see the waves curl away from the bow as our canoe surged boldly ahead towards the oblivion of that distant horizon where water and sky meet in eternity, and the lake disappears along with everything else except the vision of a distant woman; but after about half an hour, Peter's strokes were less assertive, and then they ceased altogether. I stopped paddling and turned in my seat. Peter was studying the maps, then looking around.

Art's grey canoe and Skip's green canoe had left the campsite, but were heading off in a different direction than the one Peter had chosen.

Peter picked up his paddle and continued down the lake, but his strokes became more and more tentative; then once again they stopped altogether.

More map study.

A few tentative strokes.

More study.

Eventually, he handed me the maps, and asked me if I thought he was heading in the right direction. Clearly he was, and clearly Art was not. I handed the maps back. We paddled a few more strokes, but his were without conviction. As we passed a small island, Peter suddenly swerved towards it and ran the bow up on the beach.

Eventually Art's grey canoe began to make a slow arc and headed down the lake in the direction Peter had originally gone. I urged Peter to continue, but he refused to leave the island until the others had caught up.

And so it was that on August 30th Peter and I left the expedition, and then rejoined it. Probably no one else had noticed, except perhaps Art, who was astute enough to head off in the wrong direction in order to determine just how seriously Peter wanted to be on his own.

Not that seriously. Apparently all Peter really wanted was for Art to get going a little earlier in the mornings and for all of us to stop taking so many holidays.

photo credit Robert Herendeen
An Innuit Campsite and the Whiteman's garbage dump.

Chapter Eighteen
The Garbage Dump

That evening there was a full moon. It was a lovely clear night and very cold. Art dreamed that his canoe lay overturned in a frozen basin below a rapids. In the dream his wife, Carol, was calling him home.

> September 2nd: As I dozed yesterday I had a scary dream of being on a frozen lake with men, finding the ice of the lake frozen into artifacts. One big circle, a tent ring floated loose as I stood on it; and in clear water below I could see a grey canoe (mine?) broken and resting on the bottom among caribou bones. Then Carol appeared and urged me to leave, but I continued to stand on the ice and fritter away my time. Rather a clear dream. Full moon tonight. Must get out of here soon, and will.

More than forty days earlier, back at the headwaters of the Dubawnt where his sacred tea cup (the one Carol had given him, with the rose that was all but worn off by Art's sentimental caresses) had broken on a rock, Art had had his first premonition of his approaching death and had considered turning around and returning home to Carol and his daughters.

Carol's father was a doctor who travelled in wealthy circles; Carol seemed to prefer the pleasures of cottage life on Cape Cod to those of a tent in the bush with Art and the mosquitoes. Art could hear her calling him to Cape Cod; but he lacked the resources to enter Cape Cod, except as a hired hand cleaning out the stables of the rich.

Winter was closing in; and as yet, Art had captured on film nothing that would feed his family, not on Cape Cod, not in the Green Mountains of Vermont, nor even in the bush. His only hope was to stall around waiting for something to photograph. The more he stalled, the more likely he would be able to feed his family one way or another, for he had doubled his life insurance before coming on the trip: and what people pay money to watch on television is not so much life as death.

In the equation of their desires, voices were calling Art and Carol in the same direction; but the routes by which they planned to arrive there were different. The movie provided hope for Art, hope of a reunion with his family in Vermont, half way between hell and paradise; but failing that, he preferred death in the wilderness to life in the rat race, and so when the question came up of bringing his body home, Carol replied, "He is where he wants to be, let him stay." And so Art has remained frozen in Paradise.

"Rather a clear dream," he had written in his diary.

The day he had had the dream of his broken canoe resting on the bottom among caribou bones, we were camped before another gorge, deeper and much more impassable than the first. For the next four days, wind and rain lashed our tents, before eventually turning into the more welcome snow. One gust was so strong it picked up the green canoe and rolled it to the edge of the cliff. Fortunately, Skip and Pete caught it before it was blown down the gorge.

I had pitched our tent in the most exposed position possible, to capture the spectacular view. Fortunately also, Peter had moved it to a more secure location in the lee of a ledge before the storm hit.

After waiting out the storm, we crossed the river and portaged down an esker, where caribou trails made the walking particularly pleasant.

At the beginning of the trip, Bruce and Joe had been the slowest packers, far slower than Art; but now Bruce and Joe were in good physical condition and had completed their three loads of portage before Art had completed his second. Bruce was indignant at Art's slowness.

Skip suggested to Bruce that he go hunt a caribou.

I walked back to pick up Art's last load for him and met him about half way back on the esker, studying some pebbles he had found. I showed him my pretty little tombstones, and he showed me his. We compared their beauty, and Art talked to me for a while about his daughters, for whom his pebbles were intended.

I left Art, returned to the campsite of the previous evening, and picked up his last pack; then I surveyed the ground to make sure we had left nothing behind. The esker rolled across the landscape, and there was no sign of us ever having passed over it. Nothing endured.

The following day, we came across the bear whose tracks had festooned our previous campsite. The grizzly was browsing about a hillside where puddles of water from the four-day storm were now frozen with ice. Art turned his canoe towards shore, grounded it on the rocky beach, picked up his camera and ran in pursuit.

"Say, Joe, where's your rifle?" Bruce asked, without removing his numb hands from the warmth of his pockets.

"Buried, hopelessly buried," Joe said, his cold fingers likewise searching for warmth deep in his pockets. "Where's your's Bruce?"

"Buried, hopelessly buried," Bruce repeated.

The bear, seeing Art charge up the hill, turned and charged down the hill towards him.

"Don't shoot it! FOR GOD'S SAKE DON'T SHOOT IT!" Art yelled back at us.

Arthur Moffatt is the only person I have ever met who, when confronted by a charging grizzly bear, was genuinely more concerned for the safety of the bear than for himself. Most bear lovers do their loving in front of a television set.

Skip climbed out of the stern of the green canoe with a still camera and followed Art up the hill at a respectful distance. Pete stayed with us.

"W-W-Well one of you guys had b-b-better g-g-get your r-r-rifle out," he said.

We bowmen kept our hands in our pockets. Art set up his tripod while the bear continued to charge down the hill at him.

In this game of chicken, the bear flinched first. It stopped: then it stood up to its full immense height and lifted its massive forepaws in the air. Art began filming. The bear came down on all fours and resumed its charge. While Art kept the camera rolling, the bear stopped and stood up a second time. Three times, the bear flinched. Three times, Art did not flinch. Eventually, the bear circled around more cautiously to cut off Art's line of retreat to the canoes; then it lost its nerve altogether, wheeled about and galloped hell-bent-for-election towards the far horizon. As its massive bulk crashed through shallow ponds, shards of ice, reflecting rainbow colors in the sunlight, went flying across the tundra. Great silver-tipped waves of fur rolled back and forth along its huge body as it disappeared in the distance.

With the bear out of range (Art did not have a telephoto lens; he had to take his "close-ups" close up), Art walked down the hill to the canoes as if nothing had happened.

We bowmen, with our hands still in our pockets, stared at him in disbelief.

"Weren't you scared?" Skip asked.

Art mumbled something.

He may have been afraid, but I doubt very much that it was the grizzly of which he was frightened. If his movie failed, he was as good as dead anyway.

After he died, Art's movie was shown several times on the television program "Bold Journey," where viewers nourished the Seven Deadly Sins with beer and chips. The vicarious world of television was not Art's favorite world; yet while he lived, Art had dreamed of selling his movie to this community of belly-button-popping couch-potatoes in order to buy time with his family — if not in Paradise, at least in the next best place, in the Green Mountains of Vermont.

As it grew dark at the end of the day, we saw an unfamiliar object ahead. It was a stack of cardboard boxes with cans of dehydrated vegetables inside. An empty barrel, once used to hold gasoline, stood next to the stack of boxes. A damp *Saturday Evening Post* magazine lay nearby, the pages turning in the wind. A Government topographical survey team had apparently flown in and had set up camp here not long before.

Skip admonished us for disturbing the "cache," because "caches" in the wilderness, he said, were sacred and inviolable and must never be touched. Art, however, reflected on the distinction between a cache in the wilderness and a white man's dump. We listened to Art, ignored Skip and raided the dump.

Because of the shortage of wood on Dubawnt Lake, we had used up much of our fuel for the

Coleman stove. We found some gasoline left in the big blue drum, so we topped up our five gallon tank; and Art boiled up some dehydrated spinach for supper.

After dinner, I purloined the *Saturday Evening Post* and went back to my tent to read; but I got distracted by an advertisement for "Sara Lee" frozen cheese cake. Before I knew what had happened, I was transported back to the seven deadly sins of civilization and overcome by restless longings. If only I were back in civilization, I could have all the cheese cake I could eat. I could buy a warm pair of mitts; I could sleep in a dry bed. I could join the rat race and make a lot of money, and get ulcers and commit suicide just like my father. I tossed the *Saturday Evening Post* onto Peter Franck's side of the tent, and went for a walk.

We were camped at one of the most beautiful sites I had ever seen, at the base of a sandy esker. A stream had broken through the esker on its way to joining the Dubawnt River. Up the stream, I found the skull of a musk-ox lying in a green, grassy valley.

Innuit hunters had sat on the esker hunting musk ox and caribou and fishing in the nearby lake where stream and river converged. Chipped stone knives, spear points and arrow heads of the most exquisite workmanship lay strewn about the beach. I picked up a "woman's knife," slightly fuller than a half moon in shape and delicately curved and chipped sharp for cutting meat and scraping hides. I wept in longing to be part of this lost culture, a culture that had endured in these beautiful surroundings for three thousand years by the strength of women; but now we white men had arrived and left a different type of dump behind.

The long dead Innuit, who had used the hides of the caribou to cover their kayaks, their tents, their bodies, had also used the sinews for thread, and slivers of polished bone for needles. So skilful had been their art, that their clothes were not only warm but waterproof. They tanned their leather by chewing the hide till it had become soft, then by rubbing the brains of the animal into the hide before smoking it on a smudge fire of moss.

In contrast to their tools, which were both functional and works of art, stood across the stream the ugly blue drum of gasoline — alien, giving off obnoxious vapors. It served to remind me of the values of Western Civilization from which I had wanted to escape, values which resulted in the "paving over paradise with a parking lot:" the spraying of herbicides, insecticides, fungicides on everything that lived, and blowing up the rest with nuclear devices. There was no question in my mind which culture was more beautiful; but to join the beautiful culture, I would surely have to die.

As a rule of thumb, so anthropologists say, hunting cultures like the Innuit — whose stone implements lay strewn about my feet — could support about one person per square mile. In contrast, civilized agricultures can support about one hundred persons per square mile or more. These rough figures vary from location to location. Nearer the equator, hunting cultures had once supported population densities of as high as seven persons per square mile, agricultures four hundred persons per square mile, and civilized industrial cultures, like Taiwan, a thousand persons per square mile: but here in the far north, there is not enough sunlight to support any kind of culture accept the sparsely populated Innuit, and those hunters had had to keep their numbers much lower than one person per square mile, just to keep from driving the caribou herds, upon which they depended for food, into extinction — either that, or hang around the Hudson's Bay Posts looking for a Canadian Government hand-out.

Today the population of the planet stands at about six billion and growing, which works out to be about one hundred persons per square mile, or much higher than hunting cultures can sustain. Because of the continuing growth of the human population during the last ten thousand years, hunting cultures around the world have been replaced by civilized agricultural or industrial cultures. The Innuit culture was the last hunting culture to survive in North America, but it is now gone. The white man's rifles in the hands of the southern Indians so decimated the caribou herds that the Innuit in the north either starved to death or moved to the nearest Hudson's Bay Post, where they work the electronic cash registers and watch hockey on T.V. in the evenings.

John Hornby with his young companions, Harold Adlard and Edgar Christian, had tried to go back to the hunting way of life on a beautiful location on the Thelon River: about one or two hundred miles northwest of this idyllic valley where we were now camped. And so they had followed the Innuit culture into starvation and death. The choice was clear, return to civilization or die.

photo credit Robert Herendeen
The Magnificent and Terrifying Sky.

Chapter Nineteen
Blizzard

"I-I-I th-th-think the tent is about to b-b-blow down." Peter yelled in my ear above the howling of the wind. He was trying to shake me out of a deep sleep without much success.

"Go back to sleep," I replied groggily: "it will all blow over by morning." I fell back asleep, comforted to think that God still ruled the blustering universe.

A short time later, Peter shook me again. He had already rolled up his sleeping bag and was sitting fully dressed on his air mattress, as if he were ready to abandon ship. "The t-t-tent p-p-peg on your side has p-p-pulled out," he yelled.

The wind was rising and falling in long wailing howls of about five or ten minute duration. During the peaks, the heavy nylon sides of our mountain tent snapped like the tip of a bull whip. Something was scratching and tearing at the outside of the tent next to my head

Not eager to leave the marginal warmth of my sleeping bag, I listened to the wind. The evidence clearly supported Peter's contention; the beating and clawing noises of the miscreant tent peg were definitely coming from a spot right next to my head. I looked at Peter. He was fully dressed and blowing on his hands. I wondered if he could be persuaded to go out and stick my peg back into the ground for me, but he had just come in from reinforcing his own pegs with boulders; his hands were nearly frozen from the effort. I decided there was not much hope of reasoning with him; and, anyway, I had to take a pee. I decided to kill two birds with one stone.

As I crawled out the tunnel entrance of our tent, the wind drove sleet into my bare skin. My drowsiness disappeared. When done peeing, I worked my way to windward, where the aluminum tent peg was being whipped about by the wind on the end of its two ropes. I tried to catch it in the dim dawning light. My bare feet melted the ice on the frozen gravel, and began to freeze in turn. I groped about through the wild wind for the flying tent peg, but only succeeded in getting lashed for my troubles.

Art had paid twenty dollars apiece for our three Army surplus mountain tents, and he had carried them on previous trips. Their prototypes had been tested in wind tunnels for hurricane-strength winds; but the wind tunnels had obviously not been situated on the frozen tundra, where getting a tight hold with a tent peg is difficult to do in the middle of a blizzard in the middle of the night, when one is bare naked.

Eventually, I was able to grab the miscreant peg and kick it into the gravel with a bare foot; but the ropes which held it to the tent were not tight, nor the peg well anchored. As the howling of the wind waxed, I let the wind push me back around the tent and dove through the entrance. I crawled hurriedly back into the warmth of my sleeping bag.

Before coming on the trip, I had outfitted myself with the cheapest sleeping bag available. It was made of "kapok," one of those miracle fibres which migrates to the corners of cheap sleeping bags before disappearing into the night. Having paid only six dollars for the bag, I had little enough to complain about; but I surely would have spent some cold nights, had not my mother pulled a blue woollen blanket off one of the beds at home and handed it to me as I rushed out the door to catch the plane north. Now I wrapped the woollen blanket around my shoulders and felt wonderfully warm. The sleet biting into my bare skin had caused my metabolic thermostat to race at full throttle, and the inner warmth flooded through my entire body. I fell back into the deep sleep from which Peter had not long before awakened me.

"W-W-Wake up!" Peter yelled at me.

"What's the matter now?" I asked.

"Your t-t-tent p-p-peg has c-c-come out again."

This time I took the trouble to put my boots on; but, even fully dressed, replacing the tent peg was not an easy job. The wind kept shaking the tent so ferociously that I found it impossible to hold the ropes tight while I kicked the peg into the gravel. Also, I had forgotten to pack gloves for the trip, and so the metal of the peg was cold on my bare fingers. My numb hands lacked sufficient coordination to untie the tangled ropes from the peg, and I lacked the strength to pull the ropes tight against the force of the blizzard. The wind kept jerking the peg out of my grasp. All in all, I was not having much luck securing that tent peg.

Art had provided each tent with a small canvas tarpaulin to help reduce condensation. The tarps were held away from the nylon tent by four ropes, one of which was attached to my miscreant tent peg, along with a rope leading out from my corner of the tent, which helped hold the ever-dripping wet wall of the tent away from my sleeping bag. The storm was now flailing the tent peg about at the end of these two tangled ropes like a whip. As a wave of wind peaked again to hurricane force, I fell to the ground and clutched an ice-covered rock.

Eventually, in a temporary waning of the wind, I was able to kick the peg once again into the gravel with the heel of my boot and place a few small rocks on top; but I had not been able to pull the ropes tight enough to keep the tent from snapping wildly in the wind. I hurried back inside, undressed, climbed into my sleeping bag, wrapped my blanket around me, and again fell back to sleep.

A short time later, Peter woke me again. "The t-t-tent is ripping apart," he said.

The light of dawn was coming through a long jagged tear, like a lightning bolt, on Peter's side of the tent. Strong nylon threads still held the tent together; but now as the wind rose, the snapping sounded more like a firing squad than a bull whip, and the tear became longer and longer with each explosion. Peter feared that it would not be long before the tent was a total loss, and so we agreed to strike it in order to salvage what remained and to then head out into the blizzard.

As the wind began to rise, I hurriedly dressed and rolled up my blanket and sleeping bag as Peter had already done. Peter began to crawl out through the tunnel entrance; but without his weight to hold down his side of the tent, his rolled-up sleeping bag, his air mattress and his other possessions began flying around through the air. The whole tent was flapping fiercely; and, as it continued to rise, the wind snapped the two tent poles on the northern end like match sticks. The howl reached a crescendo and the two leeward tent poles snapped in turn.

With Peter and me out of the tent, and the four tent poles broken, the wind rolled the ripped and broken remains into a ball around our air mattresses and sleeping bags. Fortunately, the tent remained tethered to the tundra by one remaining tent peg, the one Peter had secured properly with boulders.

Peter and I worked our way upwind to where the kitchen tarpaulin had once been standing. It was lying in a shambles of broken poles and wildly flapping canvas. We tried to lift it to make a shelter for ourselves, but were unsuccessful. The corners were flapping so wildly we could not maintain a grip on them for long; and the pressure of the wind was so powerful that, even when we did succeed in holding onto an edge of the canvas for a few seconds, we were unable to lift the canvas high enough to get under it.

Suddenly Art in his Moosehide jacket, his head bowed as if searching for something, appeared in a vortex of swirling sleet. We tried to exchange a few words, but the noise of the wind was too deafening. Sentences were twisted around in the cyclones and turned upside down, making them incomprehensible. I heard the word "tobacco," but could make out little else of what he was saying. As another wave of wind rolled over us, we dropped to the ground and clutched the rocks; but when we were able to stand again, Art had disappeared.

When the wind was at its strongest, breathing was difficult. Turning away from the wind, the vacuum in its wake sucked the air out of my lungs. Turning into the wind, waves of sleet were forced down my throat until I felt I was drowning. I protected my mouth with my hands and turned my head part way into the wind, and then attempted to gulp breaths of air as if from a supercharged hose.

What made survival possible at all was the rising and falling of the wind. When the tumultuous waves abated, we were able to stand and work our way into the wind towards the river where our canoe was wedged in among the rocks. Peter and I climbed under our overturned canoe, but it provided little enough shelter from the wind and none from the cold. As we lay suspended by the thwarts, our bodies began shaking uncontrollably.

We stayed in this uncomfortable position as long as we could; but when it became apparent to us that we would be frozen where we lay if we did not move, we crawled once again out from under the canoe into the full force of the blizzard. The relentless wind chilled our bodies quickly. Our only hope was to run with the wind back to our broken tent.

Once inside, Peter attempted to hold the torn nylon together with his bare hands. The howling wind reached a crescendo and tore the heavy nylon from his grasp. Everything was thrown about the tent, including Peter and me. When the wave passed, Peter resumed his grip with his left hand, and warmed his right hand in his pocket to prepare for the next onslaught. I sat cross-legged and braced the tent against the wind with my back.

I felt as if the wind, like a Greek God, was deliberately making a joke of our efforts to survive. I would have become angry, except that I felt an argument with Gods was as futile as all our other arguments; and anyway, it was clearly the fault of my carelessness that we were in this predicament.

The wind forced my head against my knees with one casual but irresistible shove.

"I give," I repeated once again, in case the wind had not heard me the first time; but it just mocked me more loudly.

Thus Peter and I tried to wait out the storm. By the time the twelfth hour had passed, I feared that the wind would never stop blowing nor the cold stop chilling, until we were frozen bent double into blocks of ice.

To distract myself from my fearful thoughts, I pulled out of my pack, during a temporary lull, a copy of the *Atlantic Monthly* and tried to read an article about the problems the Brazilians were having destroying coffee so as to keep the international price up. It took me several hours to read the short article because, every time the wind rose, I would listen to its howl.

After the gust passed, I would try to find my place and read again, but it was a slow process. Apparently, the farmers in Brazil were able to produce the coffee faster than the Brazilian bureaucracy was able to destroy it. I think the article was meant to be funny, but the humor escaped me.

Finally, I gave up on the *Atlantic Monthly* and drew from my pack Aldous Huxley's *The Perennial Philosophy*. I read a passage about becoming "one with the 'One'." It took me about four hours to read a page. As the howls increased to deafening proportions, the "One" pushed my nose into the book as if I were an un-house-trained puppy being disciplined by having its nose rubbed in its own poop.

Suddenly, Peter disappeared out the entrance of the tent without saying anything. I thought he had gone out to pee; but after a while, a box came through the entrance instead of Peter, and then another. One of the food packs came through the entrance, and then another, until the tent was so filled with packs and boxes, there was hardly any room left for us. I yelled at him that enough was enough, and eventually Peter crawled back inside and resumed holding the ripped tent without saying anything; but the stack of boxes and packs took the stress off my back, and I was able to brace myself against them and sit upright.

After waiting a while longer, Peter suggested we try to move our red canoe up from the river to further break the force of the wind. It was not an impossible idea. The canoe was upwind. All we had to do was lift it, and the wind would sail it down to the tent for us if we could hold on to it. I followed Peter out.

Once the canoe was in place and the tent weighted down with packs and boxes, Peter suggested we try once again to extricate the kitchen tarpaulin; and this time we were more successful. We anchored it to the canoe by wrapping it around the bottom and tying it to the thwarts. It was slow work because we had to do everything during lulls; but by evening, I began to feel that, thanks to Peter, we were going to survive the blizzard. And so we did.

In the morning, although the temperature of the air had fallen precipitously, and all the rocks were coated with thick ice on their northern sides, the wind had died down to mere gale strength.

Art sat all day by the fire, burning our emergency supply of driftwood in order to dry his wrung-out sleeping bag while the rest of us moved camp to a more protected location down the rapids. The air was bitterly cold. Everything was covered with ice and the wind was still blowing strongly from the north; but the blizzard had passed us by and was now visiting the weather station at Churchill, Manitoba, five hundred miles to the south, where it blew the cups off the anemometer after registering 106 miles an hour. [Hurricane strength is anything over 75 miles an hour.]

The day before the blizzard struck us, the heavens had opened up with an uncharacteristic downpour of warm tropical rain. Fat drops had drummed on the sides of the kitchen tarp and large bubbles floated on the calm river water. On that evening, two days earlier, it had felt as if we had been suddenly transported into a tropical rain forest: but appearances were deceiving. Just before the blizzard struck, the cold arctic air had forced its way beneath the warm tropical air, creating updraughts and downdraughts and chaotic cyclones which turned the rain to sleet and drove it against our tents with such terrifying force.

The evening before the blizzard struck, Art had decided to make camp and portage around a bad rapids in the morning; but the campsite had not been ideal, and we had set up our tents on an exposed plain bestrewn by boulders cemented into the glacial till. Frost heaves had left flat gravel patches large enough for each of the mountain tents; but in the early hours of the night, water had collected where Art and Joe had set up their tent. Just before the blizzard struck, the water had risen over the top of Art's air mattress and flooded his sleeping bag. He and Joe had decided to stack their two air mattresses on top of one another and had climbed together into Joe's sleeping bag. For thirty-six hours, they had lain together. They had not much liked one another before the blizzard, and cozying up to one another in Joe's sleeping bag had done little to improve their relationship.

The limit of Joe's patience arrived when Art not only moved into his sleeping bag, but into his tobacco tin as well. After Art's third cigarette, Joe put a halt to the robbery; and Art was forced out of his tent to search for his own (nearly empty) tobacco can, which he had left under the kitchen tarpaulin the evening before. When Peter and I had met him out in the blizzard, Art was searching for it.

Thirty-six hours in a sleeping bag with Joe was one thing, but thirty-six hours without a smoke was just too much for Art. He preferred to take his chances in the blizzard.

After the storm, with our tent a write-off, Art had suggested the following evening that I join Joe and him in their tent, and that Peter take shelter with Bruce and Skip. Art and Joe gave me the warm spot in the center of the tent between them. I placed my gauze-thin, six-dollar sleeping bag between Art's down mummy bag and Joe's five star Arctic sleeping bag with flannel lining separated from a canvas exterior by five pounds of the finest goose down. I smiled and never said a word: I had never been so cosy since the beginning of the trip. Obviously, the gods look after fools.

In addition to my good fortune with the warmth, Art had the oldest but best tent, the only one made out of Egyptian cotton. Egyptian cotton is stronger and lighter than nylon, and does not deteriorate in sunlight. The Army had switched to inferior nylon during the war because Egyptian cotton was not available; but the great advantage of long-fibre cotton over nylon is that it is "breatheable." Peter and I had been drenched by condensation dripping off the heavy nylon tent walls, and now I was not just warm but dry. Life was good and improving day by day.

Two days after the blizzard hit us, we had continued down the river, feeling lucky to have survived; but we had problems with ice on the canoes and on our paddle handles. I had no gloves: but even those who had them, had to remove them to melt the ice with the warmth of their bare hands, and their gloves provided little protection from either the wet spray off the bows or the cold — their gloves soon became drenched and ice formed on them. To keep their gloves dry, they paddled bare handed, and saved their dry gloves for the breaks. I had no gloves to wear on the breaks, and so my hands swelled up and turned yellow and I lost all feeling in my fingers. I feared frostbite both in my hands and in my feet, and I guess the others did too, although no one said anything; but Art took frequent breaks on shore so that we could walk around and kick the rocks to bring the circulation back to our frozen feet, and we blew on our fingers to warm them. Yet as the cold continued and the days went by, our feet swelled up, turned yellow and lost all feeling; but still we were strangely happy.

Five days later, the day Art was to die, I struggled to hold an ice-coated fish I was cleaning, but it slipped out of my numb hands. In the Army, as the most "physically fit" man in my outfit, I had won a ten-dollar bet one February by breaking through the ice and swimming across a lake. I believed that I was constitutionally stronger than other men, and therefore did not need gloves or warm sleeping bags like other mere mortals; but now my hands were so frozen that I could not perform even simple tasks like cleaning a fish. Joe took the knife from my hand and cleaned the fish for me. Not as vain as I, he had equipped himself well with the warmest sleeping bag, parka and gloves money could buy; and so the fish got cleaned.

Art cooked the fish with an inward smile, and everyone was happy and at peace: but there is a time for life and a time for death, and that day, the 14th of September, 1955, was Art's time to die, and so five days after the blizzard, Art pushed off down the river to his death.

photo credit George Luste
Just a little ripple.

Chapter Twenty
The Last Supper

Just a little ripple," Joe said, his eyes staring into space. He was lying naked on my air mattress with my blanket on top of him. I was also naked astraddle him, rubbing him down.

"Just A Little Ripple!" he repeated louder. The muscles in his neck tensed, the veins stood out. His whole body began to thrash about.

"JUST A LITTLE RIPPLE!"

I could no longer hold him down. Our one surviving tent was in danger of being destroyed by his wild and uncontrollable movements. The others were waiting patiently outside for Joe to recover his sanity. Art lay dead on the tundra, frozen. Bruce and Skip shivered in the darkness. They were perilously close to freezing also. Peter was trying to cook up some cornmeal in a tin can. The pots, pans, utensils, rifles, fishing gear, and all the food that had been in the grey and green canoes had been lost in the rapids.

"George, Pete, help!" Joe cried out.

"You're O.K. now, Joe," I said.

Every muscle in his body was struggling with death. His flailing arms bounced off me, as if he was unaware of my presence. I tried to restrain his tormented body from accidentally tearing down the tent.

"GEORGE, PETE, HELP!" he repeated.

His eyes bulged out of their sockets in terror as he looked death in the face; his motions became ever more violent.

"You are all right now, Joe," I repeated.

"GEORGE, PETE, HELP!" he yelled again.

Finally, exhausted from his struggle, Joe fell back onto the air mattress, breathing heavily. I replaced my blanket over him, straddled him once again and continued to rub him down.

"... and then we had breakfast..."

Joe began recalling the events of the day, his eyes staring blankly through the tent walls. "We stopped for lunch... (pause)."

"Yes..., yes..., we stopped for lunch, yes...."

"And then Pete caught a fish... (pause)."

"Yes..., Yes..., and Pete caught a fish...."

"And then we ate lunch... (pause)."

"Yes..., and then we ate lunch.... yes..., yes...."

"And then we continued down the river.... (pause)." Joe's eyes began to move about quickly and seemed to almost bulge out of his head. His torso began to twist and turn in an agitated manner.

"Yes..., yes..., and then we continued...."

"Just a little ripple!" he said, and propped himself up on his elbows.

"You're all right now, Joe," I repeated.

"JUST A LITTLE RIPPLE!" he yelled louder. Every muscle in his body tensed; he began to twist and turn again in agony. **"JUST A LITTLE RIPPLE!"**

"You're safe now, Joe."

"GEORGE, PETE, HELP!" he called again, completely oblivious of my presence.

For about an hour, Joe tried without success to work himself back into reality. Darkness was settling over the tundra, and the others were waiting out in the cold while his frantic agonies threatened to tear down our one surviving tent.

Joe reviewed the events of the day with ever more detail, until he came to that "little ripple" — which had turned out to be not a little ripple, but a series of cascades down which we all had been swept. When the succeeding events flooded his consciousness, his eyes stared out in terror: and he began again to struggle against the demon of death with wild flailing arms and thrashing body.

September 14th: This has been the most harrowing day of my life [Joe wrote later]. It started as many others recently: bleak and dismal under a cover of clouds. It was below freezing, and the sand was crunchy and hard from its layer of frost and ice.

Once on the river, the pleasant sandy esker country dropped rapidly behind us. We paddled along, no one saying much of anything. Finally, we pulled into a gravelly bay for lunch. George, Bruce and I scurried around looking for wood scraps, Art heated a kettle and Skip and Pete fished from the shore. Almost immediately, Pete latched onto a 17 1/2-pound orange-fleshed lake trout and wrestled with him for 20 minutes.

After a fine lunch of fish chowder, we shoved off again at around 2:30. The weather was still dismal, although the wind had dropped. In a few minutes we heard and saw rapids on the horizon....

At the top, the rapids looked as though they would be easy going, a few small waves, rocks — nothing serious. We didn't even haul over to shore to have a look, as we usually did. The river was straight and we could see both the top and foot of the rough water quite clearly, or we thought we could. We barrelled happily along. We bounced over a couple of fair-sized waves and took in a couple of splashes, but I didn't mind, as I had made an apron of my poncho and remained dry enough. I was looking a few feet in front of the canoe for submerged rocks when suddenly Art shouted "Paddle."

I took up the beat, at the same time looking farther ahead to see what it was we were trying to avoid. I was surprised to see two lines of white. I looked at them in helpless fascination. It was too late to pull to shore. Our only hope was to pick what seemed to be the least turbulent spots and head for them. I was not really frightened, but had, rather, an empty, sinking, "it's-all-over-now" feeling. We went over the falls and plunged directly into a four-foot wave. The bow sliced in, and a sheet of foaming green engulfed me. The canoe yawed, slowed. The current caught the canoe once again and plunged it toward the next falls a few hundred feet away. By some miracle, Art straightened the canoe out a little, but we were still slightly broadside as we went over the second falls.

This time the bow didn't come up. I could feel the canoe begin to roll over under me. The next few seconds telescoped into a vivid recollection of water all around me, foam and clutching currents pulling me along with the canoe, which by this time had rolled bottom up. The foaming roar stopped, the current lessened. Art and I were clinging to the canoe.

The seriousness of our position had not yet fully dawned on us. At first the water didn't feel uncomfortable. My heavy parka was full of air in between its layers, and I was quite buoyant, Art draped himself over the stern of the canoe and yelled to me to do the same at the bow. Then I saw that Bruce and Skip were in the water too, their canoe also having swamped.

The next thing I knew, George and Pete were paddling furiously by us in the red canoe, heading for shore. I watched them as they leaped out, dumped their packs and headed back toward us. Packs were floating all around us. Art was holding onto the canoe with one arm and my pack and his 86-pound camera box with the other. I saw Art's pack floating off in another direction and swam a few yards after it, but by this time my parka was soaked, so I came back to the canoe. I told Art in a dry, disinterested voice that we had just pulled a damned-fool stunt and that this would likely be the end for us. He assured me through chattering teeth that this was not the case and that, although it would be hard, we would pull through in good shape.

George and Pete went after our packs first. To our horror, as George struggled to haul my soaked pack into the canoe, he lost his balance and toppled overboard. George almost overturned the canoe trying to haul himself out of the water. That would have put all six of us in the water. None of us could have got out. Finally Pete paddled to shore, dragging George along. They dumped the water out and came back. This time they managed to drag Bruce and Skip to a small rocky island and leave them there.

By now I was almost completely paralyzed by the cold water. I couldn't swim. I couldn't move. Bruce and Skip on the island began shouting "Hurry up."

[Joe's remembrance of events at this point becomes inaccurate. Skip and Bruce were not yelling "Hurry Up!" They were yelling: "Hit me! Hit me!" to one another. It was Joe who was yelling "Hurry up."]

After lunch, Peter and I had followed Art and Joe down the river and over the falls. Like Joe, I had had that sinking "it's-all-over-now" feeling as the bow shot over the first falls and I had a glimpse of what lay below, before being knocked into a daze by that wall of green water at the foot of the first cascade. It hit me so hard I thought I was motionless while the bank zipped by me like an express train going in the wrong direction. Suddenly a second black ledge rose from the bottom of the river towards the canoe. I was jolted back to reality. I dug my blade deep into the fast moving water and feared that the handle would break. With all my strength, I propelled the canoe over the brink at full speed.

"Keep Paddling! Keep Paddling!" I yelled to Peter as the bow plunged.

Before the standing wave hit me, I braced my knees under the gunwales on each side of the canoe, and raised the paddle over my head. As we crashed through the wave, I brought my paddle down and pulled with all my strength. The bow came up. Water rolled through the canoe. I turned quickly and saw it roll out the stern behind Peter. I took another stroke as the water rolled back towards the bow, and we headed full speed towards the next ledge. With gunwales awash, we sped over the third cascade and through the rapids below. We passed Art and Joe, clinging to their overturned canoe, then crossed the basin to the nearest dry land, unloaded, and emptied the water.

Peter and I hurried back to rescue the others; but on the way, we came across Bruce's pack. I grabbed the leather straps, leaned the canoe down to the water and, using the gunwale as a fulcrum, threw my weight back and flipped the pack aboard. It was a dangerous maneuvre.

The next pack we came to was Joe's; it was bigger and heavier than the others and had been floating in the water for a longer time than Bruce's. I tried the same method, but my fingers were swollen and had long since lost feeling. The ice on the leather straps was slippery. I leaned the canoe down once again to the water, used the gunwale as a fulcrum, and threw my weight back to flip the pack aboard; but my numb fingers slipped off the ice-coated straps. Joe's pack returned to the water; I fell against the opposite gunwale. Grasping at a thwart to prevent myself from falling overboard, I saw water flooding over the gunwale into the canoe. Before the canoe tipped over, I kicked backward and somersaulted over the gunwales into the water. Peter fell to his knees, grabbed both gunwales and stabilized the canoe: but it was now once again full of water.

Five of us were now immersed in the freezing water, with only moments to live. Two of the canoes were floating upside down; the third was full of water; the provisions upon which we depended for our survival had either sunk in the rapids or were floating temporarily in the basin, or were being carried downstream by the current: and the lives of every member of the expedition depended on Peter Franck.

As I clung to the side of our canoe, Peter urged me to swim. There was an island in the basin not far away, but our progress was very slow. The sleeve of my jacket, soon sodden with water, became too heavy to lift. I kicked until I lost all feeling in my legs; soon they were dragging uselessly, weighted down by my heavy Army boots. I held onto the bow with my left arm and tried to swim on my back with all my remaining strength, but our progress was painfully slow.

I decided I would have to remove my clothes if I were to be of any help to Peter, which was a mistake. When I unzipped my jacket, the icy water flooded around my chest and cramped my muscles. I could not breathe. Desperately, I tried to pull my chest out of the water: and, once again, I nearly tipped the canoe over. I looked at Peter and saw terror in his face; he fell to his knees and tried to stabilize the canoe. Climbing aboard was out of the question. I fell back and tried to swim again, until my arm became so tired I could not lift my sodden sleeve out of the water. I was clearly more of a hindrance to Peter than a help.

I had always imagined myself performing a self-sacrificing act at the moment of death. So I let go of the canoe to enable Peter to reach the island. My heavy Army boots dragged me down, and the icy water closed over my head.

Looking death in the face, I changed my mind. Being a hero was one thing, but dying was something else. I decided I was not the self-sacrificing type after all. I fought my way back to the surface, recovered my grip on the gunwale, and once again tried to swim while the icy water swirled through my open jacket and drained the remaining strength from my body.

"Keep Swimming, Keep Swimming," Peter urged. I looked up at him. He was so close, and yet so far away. His eyes were filled with horror. He was not looking at me, but staring at something ahead. I turned and saw the island moving away from us. The canoe was in current. We were being swept passed the island downstream to a certain death. With my last remaining strength, I redoubled my efforts: but my legs were useless, my right arm nearly so, and the sodden sleeve of my jacket too heavy to lift. There was no hope. Peter's only chance of survival depended on me letting go of the canoe. Once again I sank to the bottom, but this time not nearly so far.

"I can touch. I can touch." I yelled joyfully, my head just emerging from the water. I held the canoe against the force of the current, and Peter worked the canoe towards the island. As my body came out of the water, I tried to walk; but with no feeling in my legs, I was forced to crawl instead.

After emptying the canoe, Peter helped me back in. He handed me my paddle. I had no feeling in my hands. I dropped it. He picked it up and handed it to me again. I dropped it again. The third time, I stared at my fingers and gripped the paddle with all my strength. I could no longer feel where my hands were, but I could still see them. I told them what to do as if I were operating a robot.

I threw my shoulders forward and watched my arms, dangling like leather straps, follow. When the blade struck the water, I pulled with all my strength. The canoe surged forward once again.

The more I paddled, the more I recovered, and soon I was a help to Peter; but icy wind continued to blow through my open jacket, cooling my skin and drawing the life-giving warmth from me.

At first, Peter headed towards the grey canoe, with Art hanging onto its stern and Joe onto the bow. The grey canoe had been the first to capsize. Art and Joe had been in the water the longest, but before we reached them, we heard other voices calling: "George, Pete, Help!" Words that Joe would repeat over and over again in his approaching delirium.

We abandoned Art and Joe and turned to rescue Skip and Bruce first. They were clinging to their overturned green canoe as it was being swept out of the basin downstream.

"George, Pete, Help!" Skip and Bruce cried again. We raced to catch them before they were swept away.

As we came alongside, I yelled at them to hold onto the stern of our canoe behind Peter, and we would drag them to a second island further downstream. Skip held onto the overturned green canoe as well as to ours, and we ran with the current down to the island, where they crawled out onto dry land.

"Hit me! Hit me!" Skip yelled.

"Hit me! Hit me!" Bruce yelled back. They stood facing one another. Water dripped off Bruce's parka and Skip's yellow "slicker." They had difficulty making their arms move. They twisted their shoulders; their arms followed, and soon they were able to bring some feeling back to their arms.

"Hit me! Hit me!" they continued to chant.

Peter turned our canoe upstream, and we dug our paddles into the fast water to rescue Art and Joe. Our paddle handles bent, but our progress was slow against the current, and I was nearing the point of total exhaustion.

"Hurry up, hurry up," I heard Joe yell in his husky voice through chattering teeth. Neither he nor Art had called out before, not even when we had turned away from them to rescue Skip and Bruce. Their heavy parkas had protected them from the icy water at first, but now I heard Joe's voice yelling more desperately as the cold penetrated to his skin and carried away the life-sustaining warmth. Ice water against the skin draws off body heat about eighty times faster than air; it can kill a man in about twenty minutes. Their time had nearly run out, and they were only partly conscious.

By the time Peter and I brought our canoe alongside, Art and Joe could only stare up at us with blank and uncomprehending eyes. We instructed them, as we had instructed Skip and Bruce, to hold onto our canoe at the stern behind Peter.

Art let go of the overturned grey canoe and held onto our gunwale, but his other hand still gripped tightly his heavy pine camera chest, which held nine thousand feet of film and all his camera equipment. This chest was the means by which he hoped to feed his family: and of this hope he would not let go, even as death came upon him.

Joe grabbed onto our canoe at the stern next to Art, but he would not let go of the over-turned grey canoe. Peter and I strained every muscle, but our progress was slow.

"Let go of the grey canoe!" Peter urged Joe.

My mind became fogged. [Joe wrote later.] I remember Pete shouting to me to grab hold of his canoe. [Pete was shouting at him to let go of the grey canoe.] I did. So did Art. I was holding onto Art's pack. [He had let go of Art's pack and was holding onto both canoes.]

We got nowhere, although George and Pete paddled like fiends. I lost my grip on Pete's gunwale and shouted for him to come back or I would drown. He quickly stopped paddling. I grabbed onto the red canoe again.

The next thing I remember, my feet were scraping over the rocks near shore. I took one or two steps using every single remaining ounce of strength I had, then collapsed unconscious on the rock and moss shore.

Totally exhausted, I fell out of the bow seat and crawled onto the island alongside Art and Joe. None of us could walk. I lay beside them.

Peter urged me to get back into the canoe to pick up Bruce and Skip downstream. I said I couldn't, and he left without me. Joe lay on the tundra. Art knelt on the gravel and fumbled with the zipper of his Moosehide jacket, trying to get his clothes off: but he had lost all feeling and coordination in his fingers. "What do you want me to do?" he asked.

There was one pack on the island, Bruce's pack. It had been the first pack Peter and I had rescued before my unsuccessful attempt to haul Joe's oversized pack aboard. Peter had left it on the island after dumping the water out of the canoe when we had arrived at this island the first time. I crawled over to it, pulled down on the leather straps to release the buckles, and hauled out Bruce's sleeping bag. I dragged it over to Art and together we tried to get our clothes off. I was slightly more successful than Art. The zipper on my jacket was already undone, but I lacked the coordination to undo the buttons on my shirt.

"What do you want me to do?" Art repeated, while fumbling unsuccessfully with the zipper on his Moosehide jacket.

"Get undressed, and get in this sleeping bag with me," I repeated.

Unable to undo the buttons on my shirt, I thrust my fingers through the opening, clenched my fists, threw back my shoulders and ripped every button off. The icy wind sliced into my wet long johns.

"What do you want me to do,?" Art repeated helplessly a third time.

"Get undressed and get into this sleeping bag with me," I answered ritualistically; but my consciousness was now focused almost entirely on my own survival. I ceased to be aware of Art or of anything else, except the cold wind slicing into my wet long johns and drawing the heat of life from my body. I thought of only one thing: escape. I crawled into Bruce's sleeping bag.

Contrary to popular opinion, freezing to death is not a pleasant way to die. It is so painful, in fact, that I desperately wanted to pass out, to go crazy or (failing that) to die as quickly as possible. During waves of consciousness, my mind raced over the possibilities of making a fire, finding food, or of rescue. I had thought about the Royal Canadian Air Force miraculously landing on the basin, or a band of Innuit hunters stumbling unexpectly upon us. The chance of this happening was so clearly remote that I soon despaired of survival, and only desired to get rid of the pain as quickly as possible. As Oscar Wilde once remarked: "I don't mind dying, I just don't want to be there when it happens."

I did my best to escape reality, by one means or another; but that was not as easy as it might sound. I was like an insomniac trying to sleep: the pleasant dreams would not come until I had sincerely accepted the inevitability of death. Then they came, but they did not stay. They were so pleasant that they revived my will to live. When first I regained consciousness, the cold, instead of being painful, was ecstatically pleasurable. It reminded me that I had not yet died. Where there is life, there is hope; and my mind raced once again over the possibilities of rescue. Then the hope faded and turned to despair; the pleasure turned to pain; my only desire was to die as quickly as possible, and then the dreams came again.

In the first dream, I had been walking through the woods of New Hampshire on a pleasant Autumn day with the sun pouring down upon me through the orange and red leaves of the maple trees. My second dream was of sitting by a fire in Zaidee's apartment.

Between dreams, before the despair set in once again, I had time to reflect. I reflected on the meaning of death. I tried to visualize my obituary in the paper:

"George James Grinnell, age 22, died September 14th, 1955 on a damned fool expedition to the Arctic."

I thought about God. Did I believe that God would save me? Hardly! I had more faith in a rescue attempt by the Royal Canadian Air Force, and my faith in that was about as minimal as it gets.

I asked myself if I was glad to have come on the expedition. I was very glad. I preferred to die in that lovely Garden of Eden, rather than to have lived my four score and ten in the other world from which I had at last escaped. Better death in the wilderness than life in civilization; yet when I passed out, it was of civilization that I dreamed.

In my third dream, I was lying sick in bed as a child of about five, and my mother was bringing food up to me. She was calling out, "George, George, are you all right," which I had thought was strange, because my mother had always called me "Jim."

Skip and Bruce had recovered enough to help Peter paddle the red canoe back upstream. They had taken time to pick up a bag of emergency driftwood along the way and to secure Art's pack still floating in the basin. By the time they returned to the island Art, Joe and I were on, the three of us were unconscious.

They undressed Art and put him in a sleeping bag. Peter, the only man who had not fallen in the water, was also, ironically, the only man who carried his matches in a waterproof container. He lit a small fire with our emergency driftwood. He helped Skip move Art near it, and attempted to give Art artificial respiration. Then they removed Joe's clothing, all except his wet long johns, and carried him over to where I was having pleasant dreams.

"George, George, are you all right?" I heard in my dream.

Suddenly I awoke and remembered that I had left Art and Joe out in the cold.

"Yes, I'm fine," I answered; but when I realized my selfishness, I longed to escape once again into that other, more pleasant, dream world. The cold was difficult enough to deal with, but facing my cowardly betrayal of Art and Joe was too much reality for me to handle.

Joe's foot kicked me in the face.

"We are putting Joe in with you," Skip said.

Joe's delirious, kicking and thrashing body reminded me that he was in far worse pain than I was; and I began rubbing him down.

My next recollection [Joe continues], hazy as it is, is one of being in a sleeping bag, with George giving me a brisk rubdown. He kept asking, "How are you doing, Joe?" and I kept telling him that I was doing fine and to quit pounding me. I remember that I felt warm and comfortable all over except for my feet, which seemed abnormally cold.

Outside, I could hear Pete and Skip talking in a worried fashion about Art. They had rescued his pack and the emergency sack of driftwood; they had undressed him and put him in his sleeping bag by

215

the little fire that Peter had built. They tried to bring him around, but he had not responded, and neither knew what to try next.

After a while, I crawled out of the sleeping bag Joe and I shared, and asked Skip if he wanted me to get in with Art and try to rub him down. Skip was distraught and grateful for my offer to help. He was still fully dressed in his wet clothing. His yellow water-proof slicker provided some protection against the wind: but his teeth were chattering, and he kept moving about so as not to freeze.

Before I climbed in with Art, I asked him to help me pull my wet underwear off. Naked, I at last felt warm, though the temperature of the air was well below freezing and the wind bitterly cold.

Art's naked body was cold to the touch and seemed very frail. The side next to the fire was warmer than the other side. After a few minutes, I began to wonder if he was being warmed by the fire or being cooked. Eventually, I had to face the fact that he was dead. I lingered with him for a little longer, my naked body trying to pass some warmth to his naked body: but he lay very still.

Skip and Pete set up the one surviving tent, removed Joe's long johns and placed his tormented body on my air mattress with my blanket on top of him, which he repeatedly kicked off in his struggles. There being little more that could be done, Bruce repaired to his sleeping bag, so as not to add another unconscious body in the growing darkness.

Skip was nearing the end of his strength. I emerged from Art's sleeping bag and asked him if he wanted me to go in with Joe to rub him down. He readily agreed, and so I sat astraddle Joe, naked body to naked body, and rubbed his chest.

Every time Joe recalled the events of the day, he would come to that "little ripple" and go crazy, his arms flailing about uncontrollably, his eyes wide with terror, until, as darkness spread over the tundra, I feared he would tear our one remaining tent down: but finally he tried a different tack and began to recall backwards the events of the day.

"We had lunch..., and before that, Pete caught a fish... (pause)."

He seemed calmer. He was staring up at the tent ridge, concentrating hard.

"Yes, yes, and before that Pete caught a fish...."
"...and before that we passed out of the pleasant esker country... (pause)."

"Yes...," I encouraged, "and before that...."
"...and before that, we had breakfast...."

Suddenly, Joe sat bolt upright and stared in horror at my naked body astraddle him.

"George! What are you doing!"
"You are O.K. now, Joe," I said.

"Jesus Christ! George! Get off me!" He pushed me off. His shove was purposeful and with force. Before, when he had been thrashing about, his arms had frequently struck me; but it was as if he was unaware of my presence. He had recognized me at last. I knelt beside him. He looked around the tent, and then at my blanket on top of him, a puzzled expression on his face.

"You're O.K. now," I repeated, fearing that he would retreat into the relative safety of insanity yet again when he realized where he was.

"Where's Art?" he asked.

"Art's outside," I replied.

"I just had the most terrible dream," he said.

"You're all right now," I said.

He stared at me for a long time, as if he were trying to make sense of things, then he said: "It wasn't a dream was it?"

"You're O.K. now," I repeated.

"Thanks, George," he finally said, and rolled over on his side. Just before falling into a deep sleep, he mumbled, "You can have all my tobacco, George."

All his tobacco had been lost to the river.

When I came around next [Joe continues], I was surprised to find that I was completely naked and in a tent. I couldn't figure out why this would be. I sat bolt upright. It was dark out. Someone [Peter Franck] thrust a large can under my nose and told me to take five swigs. I did. Then Skip came into the tent, undressed and got into a sleeping bag. After a while, I looked out of the tent. I turned back and casually asked Skip where Art was. He replied that Art was outside. We lay in silence. Finally, I asked what would Art be doing outside. Skip replied, "You might as well know, Art is dead."

From the food supplies which had survived in the red canoe, on the fire he had built out of our emergency sack of driftwood (which we had diligently collected whenever a brook had come down to the river carrying its precious little gifts), Peter had cooked up some corn meal in a tin can and had bent the lid for a spoon. Bruce and I joined Skip and Joe in the tent, and Peter passed the tin can full of hot corn meal in to us. We handed the mush first to Joe.

Taking the bent tin lid, Joe made one of his expert scoops and scored a large lump; but instead of gulping it down, he passed it to Bruce on his right. Bruce looked at it, and offered it to Skip. Skip looked at it, and handed it to me.

In the beginning of the trip, I had taken comfort in believing that I would not be the first man to die, because I was in the best physical condition; but now as I stared at that lump of corn meal, I had other desires. I passed the enticing lump back to Joe, who ate it, then Joe passed the whole can of corn meal over to Bruce.

What we had all learned was that there are things more frightening than death. What we passed around that night was more than just a can of lumpy mush. "Take, eat; this is my body which is given for you: do this in remembrance of me...."

When the corn meal was gone, Peter passed in a package of Velveeta cheese. I handed it to Skip. He took out Art's hunting knife and sliced the cheese into six equal pieces and then passed them around for us to choose, as was his custom. When the cheese came back to him, he picked up the fifth piece, and we all stared at the sixth remaining piece. Art lay outside. We all wondered if we should bring him into the tent with us and give him his piece of cheese, even though he was now dead.

Finally, Skip divided up the sixth piece: but once again, he divided it into six pieces. Then, at last, he divided up the sixth morsel five ways, and we finished off all the cheese, leaving none for Art.

That night, the five of us huddled into the tiny two-man mountain tent. The shivers and the shakes rolled from one side of the tent to the other as we shared what little warmth remained between us.

photo credit George Luste
The Dubawnt River

Chapter Twenty-One
The Test

The next day, I knocked the ice off my buttonless Army shirt and put it on to thaw. All the packs that had ended up in the water were frozen solid. Before we could get at their inner contents, we had to break the ice by banging them on the rocks. The only way to dry our frozen clothing was to put it on and to let our bodies thaw everything out.

I sat on a rock to rest. Art's stiff body lay on the tundra next to me. He did not seem dead. Death is separation, and Art was not separate. Our families and friends back in civilization were separate. They were dead, but Art was still with us. Skip was nearby, knocking the ice out of Bruce's frozen clothing. The others were still in the tent.

I felt at peace. I also felt great affection for Skip, who had awakened me from my sleep of death the day before.

The sun came out and warmed me. I sat on a rock and basked in it and stared at a dwarf birch leaf in a clear pool of water by my feet. It seemed incredibly beautiful. Then I saw Skip turn and walk towards me. I was glad of his company. I wanted to tell him that he had been right all along about "group consideration and altruistic behavior" and about all things that he believed in. I was glad to be alive, but I wished I had not left Art out in the cold to die.

When Skip came near, I smiled up at him; but instead of smiling back, he looked down at the ground as if at a loss for words. I thought he was preparing another lecture on "group consideration and altruistic behavior," but he was looking for other phrases.

Finally, he said: "You were right all along, George."

"I have never been right about anything in my entire life," I replied.

"At 'the moment of truth' I had always thought I would have done the courageous thing."

I looked at him with a puzzled expression on my face.

"If I had not called out, you would have rescued Art first."

"We picked you and Bruce up because your canoe was in current."

"I should not have called out," he repeated.

"I should not have crawled into Bruce's sleeping bag."

He paused, then looked down: "I just came over to thank you for saving my life."

"You are welcome. Thank you for saving mine," I replied.

Art lay dead on the tundra next to us.

"It is because of me, not you, that Art is dead," he said and turned away. Then he paused and turned toward the sun. "I can understand why 'primitive' people worshipped the sun."

The wilderness around us filled us both with awe. On the one hand, we were terrified of it: on the other hand, its beauty elevated us to a plateau of sublime peace.

Skip spent the remainder of the day knocking the ice off other people's clothing, drying everything on his own body.

photo credit Skip Pessl
The Last Farewell

Chapter Twenty-Two
The Last Farewell

According to the best Buddhist authorities, sooner or later everyone becomes "enlightened." For most of us, it is later rather than sooner. In the last moment before death, the sensation of falling down a bottomless black hole into oblivion is followed by a blinding light and a feeling of warmth. The seven deadly sins of inner discontent fall away; the Angels start singing, and despair is turned into gratitude for all that was, for all that will ever be, for the eternal union with God.

Not everyone dies at the moment of enlightenment. Soldiers in battle have fallen into the abyss and survived to tell about it, and so have patients in hospitals. Enlightenment can come in strange places at strange times. It can also be induced through pilgrimage. Pilgrims have a physical destiny, such as the birthplace of a saint; but the real voyage is travelled within one's soul.

On their pilgrimage, Christian monks use as their vehicle the death of Jesus. They become Jesus as Jesus descends into the black abyss of hell, and then rises to the realm of golden light to become one with God and the angels everlastingly.

Buddhist monks, on the other hand, "meditate" rather than "contemplate," a distinction which achieves the same end. On a three-month meditation, Buddhist pilgrims will retire to a cell and let all thoughts pass through consciousness until the sensation of falling into the abyss descends upon them. Like the Christian monks, they will experience fear, anxiety, and finally despair; but if they have worked hard on their meditation and have successfully emptied themselves of their own desires, they will become that grateful empty vessel through which the grace of God flows.

In the presence of a bodhisatva, one feels the love of God flowing out to one; it is a very peaceful feeling. At some point in his life, either in the war or in the wilderness, Art had become a bodhisatva.

As Art travelled through the passages of life, he had been torn between his two homes, the home where his family lived and his spiritual home in the wilderness. It is difficult to walk, as Art tried to walk, in both worlds at once.

We had no idea how long it would take us to reach the outpost at Baker Lake: and it was clear that we were now critically short of food, as most of our emergency rations had been lost to the falls. Joe and Bruce had also lost their rifles, so we would be hunting no more caribou; and the only fishing rod to survive was Peter's, but Peter had only one lure left.

We did not have time to linger. We carried Art's frozen body to the top of the hill and turned his grey canoe over him. Skip suggested that we take a minute to say our last farewell.

It is now forty years later, September 15th, 1995, and I am still trying to say farewell. I owe Art a debt I cannot express. He had understood something about the wilderness, and he had done his best to share his understanding with us.

Art never preached, but he had made the pilgrimage before. He took me to the Garden of Eden where I could meet his God. He made me feel lucky to be alive, and I am eternally grateful.

My seven deadly sins of civilization had fallen away on that pilgrimage. When I had been a glutton, my belly had been full, but I had not felt satiated. When I had been slothful, I had taken plenty of rest, but still I felt tired. When I had been avaricious, I had collected many possessions, but yet I wanted more. When I had been lustful, I had had enough sex, but still I felt frustrated. When I had been vain, I had never felt sufficiently appreciated. My seven deadly sins had all been sins of inner discontent. The discontent made me feel angry; angry at the world, angry at my fellow creatures, angry at myself; and so I had not been happy, and I had not made others happy: but on Art's pilgrimage into the Garden of Eden, the seven deadly sins had fallen away from me — and by the time Art died, I only felt gratitude, gratitude for the caribou, gratitude for the love of my companions, and gratitude for the peace I felt within.

This was the gift I had received on Art's pilgrimage. No greater gift can a person receive.

When Saint Anthony had rested in the wilderness for all but the first eighteen of his ninety years, Saint Anthanasius had given him a sheep skin rug to lie on. Before that, he had slept on the stone floor of his cave on nothing more than his hair shirt; and yet, he too had found peace.

At the age of eighteen, Saint Anthony had given away his inheritance: and when he died at the age of 104, his will was a simple one. He left his hair shirt to the monk in the cave to his right, and his sheep skin rug to the monk in the cave on his left. He had not possessed much: but, divested of the seven deadly sins, he had been filled with the grace of God.

Art had taken us to that same spiritual place in the Garden of Eden where Saint Anthony, and so many other pilgrims, had found peace.

Enlightenment comes from looking at the wilderness, the creation, with eyes of awe. It is not something that comes through reason or through study at a university, because enlightenment is not knowledge, but a change in perspective; and so Art did not preach. He waited until we were able to see that the wilderness is not an enemy to be conquered, but a gift to be loved. Art understood that enlightenment is a "gestalt shift" in which the World is viewed differently.

Jesus did not spend time at a university, he spent time in the wilderness.

And at once the Spirit drove him into the desert, and he remained there for forty days, and was put to the test by Satan. He was with the wild animals, and the angels looked after him. (Matthew, 4:11)

Jesus's parables are about seeing the world from a different perspective, not about the Gross Domestic Product.

What I learned from Art is that God, if there is a God, is not an object so much as a relationship — the reconciliation of all things to all things. When I feel reconciled to God, I feel awe for the gift of Creation, I feel love for my fellow creatures, and I feel peace within myself. This is the gift Art shared with us.

Later I was to learn of another aspect of God, the transcendental one. The spirit of God is in all things: but morality, which transcends the natural desires, comes from a different source.

If one takes seriously Socrates's injunction to "know thyself," one will eventually come to the understanding that we have done things we ought not to have done, and we have left undone those things which we ought to have done, and that we are not worth dying for. It is not "reasonable" that Jesus or Art or the caribou or any other creature should die for us.

We are very reasonable creatures: but to feel the grace of God, one must forget about reason and go on a pilgrimage to a place where we no longer "see as through a glass darkly," to a place where we are able to see the death of a caribou or a chicken with eyes of gratitude, rather than with eyes of conquest. Art had taken us on a pilgrimage to that holy place, the Garden of Eden which resides within our souls.

Jesus had spent forty days in the Wilderness, Saint Anthony a lifetime; but for us, seeing the world from a different perspective had taken about three months. It had not been until our second forty days that we had begun to feel grateful instead of angry.

Gratitude came first in the form of appreciation for small favors, small favors which we now understood to be not so small, the gift of rain, the gift of the sun, the gift of the life of a caribou which had died for us.

"The lilies of the field, they toil not, neither do they spin, yet the good Lord provides for them all;" and so the good Lord had provided for us as well. With the growing sense of gratitude came a growing sense of love: love for the creation, love for one another, and love for the grace of God which made us feel so peaceful.

We had come to realize that although life is very short, it is very precious: and we understood that when Art died, he was not separated from us and from the Creation, but one with us, one with all things.

We placed Art's body under his canoe on the top of the hill. We could not bury him because the ground was frozen and we had no shovels.

After a moment of reflection, which has lasted forty years, we turned and continued down the hill.

How many times I have gone down the hill, fallen back into the seven deadly sins of discontent, lost that sense of gratitude Art had led me to. How many times I have tried to tell this story truthfully. How many times I have failed.

photo credit Richard Irwin
Balanced Gently

Chapter Twenty-Three
Flies of the Lord

To the East, the dawning Arctic sky was playing a concert in color. Through blue holes in the lower layers I saw wispy cirrus clouds of ice sparkling like diamonds in the golden light of the rising southern sun. Closer to the earth, the darker clouds burned crimson above the azure horizon while to the north, all was swallowed up in threatening blackness. Everything was still. My feet crunched the moss as I walked to our little fireplace and began building the morning fire.

This was the day of the autumnal equinox. The sun was over the equator far south of us. At the summer solstice, when the sun had reached its most northern extent a quarter of a year earlier, we had entered this sublime northern world. Day in day out, week in week out, month in month out, we had paddled towards that distant oblivion, never quite reaching it physically, but becoming transformed by it spiritually, and here I was in a place of perfect beauty.

I laid the fire carefully, dry tinder upon a crumpled square of toilet paper, the tips of three tarp poles pointing with the wind, a fourth and fifth laid across them to provide control of the draft. There was no wood about, and we had lost our stove in the falls, but Art had provided us well with those long spruce poles he had cut early in the trip; they had held up the tarp, now they provided fuel for the fire.

When the water in the tin cans began to boil, Bruce appeared from the tent and began to cook up one of his gourmet concoctions. He had outdone himself this past week since Art had died.

At the end of a long portage that had saved us about a hundred miles of river travel, he had fed us a memorable stew consisting of mouldy oatmeal, peanut butter laced with slivers of glass, spinach we had liberated from the Survey crew's dump, and the remains of a fish Peter had caught. It may not sound so good, but truly I experienced it as the most delicious meal I have ever eaten.

Bruce had done his best to remove the larger slivers of glass from the peanut butter. Some weeks earlier, a box had come open on a portage; a peanut butter jar had smashed on a rock, and slivers of glass had stuck to it. Peter had gone back and scraped the peanut butter off the rock and saved it for an emergency ration, which we now appreciated.

Bruce did not have much food nor any pots to work with, but he took great pains and somehow he managed to produce the most delicious meals we had eaten during the entire trip. The box of spices had survived the falls because they had been in the red canoe, and Bruce used them with creative imagination to disguise the flavor of mouldy macaroni.

As he busied himself by the fire, the killer instinct in Bruce seemed to have passed, as it had passed in all of us. He had lost both his rifle and his fishing rod to the falls, and he did not seem to miss them. Rather he seemed happy that he no longer had to kill. The days of Bruce as thrill-seeking sportsman were gone. He spent his days dreaming of ways to please our palates with whatever little food that had remained from the red canoe. Sitting in the position of leadership by the fire where Art and Skip had once sat, he was the happiest I had ever seen him.

Neither Art, when he had been cook, nor Bruce now that he was cook, had any real desire to control the men. They did, however, have different visions of how the expedition should be run. Bruce had organized his previous revolt well.

Bruce believed in consensus. He had always asked us our opinions; had organized our opinions; and then he had led the revolt against Art. Bruce had appointed me the spokesman for his United Bowmen's Association because I was the eldest of the bowmen, but I was neither the organizer nor the force behind the bowmen's revolt. When matters had come to a head at the gorge, I had preferred to sit beside Art in the wet, cold end of the tarp, than by Bruce by the fire; and in the end so had the others.

Art did not lead by consensus. He only twice asked us our opinions. On the evening of August 3rd, he had asked us if we wanted to turn back, and a second time three weeks later, when we had been wind-bound on Dubawnt lake, he had asked us for our opinions about what was to be done; perhaps he was then attempting to forestall another major rebellion like the one at the gorge where we had been immobilized by the weather for four days, but generally speaking Art let us go our way, and he went his. On the two times he had asked our opinions, our answers had been the same: "Get up before dawn and paddle rain or shine as fast as possible for Baker Lake," which is probably why he so rarely asked our opinions. There is a journey of the body, and a journey of the soul. We could not understand the journey Art's soul had embarked on, balanced gently as he was like a bird on the arctic horizon.

After he died, we moved as we had always wanted to move: as fast as possible to the safety of Baker Lake. We left the island on which Art lay dead at noon on September 16th, and arrived at Baker Lake at noon eight days later, a distance of 250 miles; and, one of those eight days, we had been held up by a blizzard. After Art died, we travelled four times faster than when he was alive and set a record for fast canoe travel in the north.

Art's destination had not been Baker Lake, and he never arrived there. He was trying to make a movie of the wilderness which would both earn enough money to feed his family, and at the same time capture the beauty of the wilderness in a manner he had experienced it. He failed in both attempts, but he died trying: and we nearly died willingly with him.

On that fateful day, Bruce had cried out. Skip had cried out. Joe had cried out. I had crawled into Bruce's sleeping bag to save myself. Art had gone silently into that dark night, slowly freezing to death, while clinging onto to his camera chest with nine thousand feet of wet film inside, the symbol of his love for his family.

We had rebelled against Art's leadership: his willingness to risk his life and ours for the love of his family, his endless delays, his futile quest to capture on film that which can not be captured on film.

Bruce had been the real leader of our revolt, but when matters had come to a head, and we were forced to choose between Bruce and Art, we had chosen to follow Art and not Bruce for reasons which are not altogether explicable. What Bruce represented was our untrammeled desire to save our own skins. What Art represented was that elusive vision that transcends even life itself.

Bruce understood what is worth living for. Art understood what was worth dying for.

Art had volunteered for the American Field Service assigned to the British Eight Army in Africa, not to kill (he refused to carry a gun), but to die for what he had believed worth dying for at the time. He had become disillusioned, and had escaped into the wilderness, but once again he carried no gun. He preferred to be killed by wild animals than to kill them; but, in the end, his real desire was simply to feed his family in such a way that he did not have to destroy parardise or blow up other human beings. And so Art gave us a choice: follow Bruce and kill rather than be killed, or lay down our lives for the life of the Creation.

Like Art, Bruce had not attempted to tell us what to do. He had only asked us to express our feelings, and then he had tried to organize those feelings into concerted action.

I felt scared. I wanted a more rigorous schedule that would ensure our safe arrival at Baker Lake as quickly as possible. I was happy to be part of the United Bowmen's Association. I had acted as spokesman for the UBA and had challenged Art's leadership as an instrument of Bruce's rebellion, but I had also hesitated. There was something compelling about Art's quest; that search for whatever it is that is not just worth living for, but also worth dying for. We were uneasy in our youth, but we too wanted to become birds on the edge of the arctic sun.

Although Skip had not much cared for us bowmen, for our pursuit of our own interests, appetites and passions, he too had had moments of weakness, moments of anger; he too had cried out to be rescued when faced with the reality of death. He too had been an instrument of Bruce's rebellion, but he was not proud of his weakness. He too wanted to be like Art, so noble, so wise. He wanted something worth dying for, but when faced with death, he knew, I knew, we had not found it. And so we wavered, disciples of Art, instruments of Bruce's rebellion. In the end, we had saved ourselves, and now Bruce sat by the fire in Art's place, cooking up far more delicious meals than Art had ever cooked. Skip and I stood with our heads down, staring at the ground while we ate those delicious meals in silence, then boarded our canoes and paddled as fast as we could for Baker Lake.

After Art's death, Skip had suggested that he and Peter take one of the canoes and paddle quickly to Baker Lake to bring back help. Joe, Bruce and I, the three bowmen, were to be left on the island with Art's body; but we bowmen were disinclined to sit around and wait to be rescued. We decided that we would take a canoe and continue on our way regardless of what Skip and Pete wanted to do, so Skip relented and we all decided to travel together; and after that day there were no bowmen, and no sternmen, and no leader, just the five of us travelling together across the beautiful land as fast as possible.

I still had the only watch in camp, so it was natural for me to rise before dawn, wake the others and start the breakfast fire. Nobody told me to, nobody told me not to. We seemed to fall into various jobs around camp and were happy for whatever help we could be to the group as a whole. Because all our pots and pans were lost to the river, Bruce could no longer cook as Art had cooked, by hanging the pot's bail handle on a stick over the fire. At meal time I gathered stones on which to rest the tin cans; and, while Bruce brewed up his delicious concoctions, I tended the fire and steadied the cans with my frozen hands.

What causes some frozen fingers to fall off and others to stay on is not for me to say, because I am not a doctor and I do not know the answer; but I believe circulation is the key. I have heard of Buddhist monks walking barefoot on the glaciers of the Himalayas while Western mountain climbers, their feet laced up tight in climbing boots, have lost their toes. I believe that the swelling of frozen hands and feet in the cold is nature's way of protecting them, and that tight boots are dangerous because the circulation is cut off to the toes once the feet start to swell. Fortunately our civilized boots had all fallen apart by this time, and so our circulation ran free. Although I had lost all feeling in my hands, and they were yellow and swollen, I suffered more from burns than from frostbite. Earlier in the cold weather, my hands had frozen and thawed, frozen and thawed, but now they just stayed numb all the time. Earlier the paddling had thawed them out, and when feeling returned, it returned with great pain. The pain was now gone, and my fingers remained on my hands. The swelling seemed to be insulating the vital functions beneath the skin. Nature had forgiven me one more time. Without gloves, the miracle of physiology protected me instead.

Tending the fire was the best job in camp. I am not quite sure how I ended up with the job, but I was the only man without gloves, and my hands were in the worst shape. I had no feeling in my fingers which was both an advantage and a disadvantage. They were pain-free when I burned them, but I noticed a growing number of black scars. It felt good to be close to the fire. It felt better to know that, yet once again, the others were silently taking care of me, letting me have a job close to the fire to help nature keep my fingers attached to my hands.

On one level, we had abandoned Art, left his body on the island; but Art's pilgrimage had inwardly changed us all, not just physically through frozen feet, but spiritually. Joe, once the slothful complainer, now passed choice morsels of food to others. With the best gloves in camp, he was the one who now cleaned the fish Peter caught, a nasty job in an arctic wind with ice forming on their slippery skin because the gloves had to be removed to melt the ice to get a firm grip. Every one in camp tried to be helpful in a quiet way, but none more than Joe. Once the slowest man on the portages, Joe was now the one to pile on the heaviest loads.

Skip retained his self-denial, his hard work, but the arrogance was gone. No one was more humble than Skip. The lectures were gone; he never told us what to do, never had to. He just worked harder than everyone else as he had always done. We shared with him now the same desires; the desire to do something for others, the desire to be of some help to the group as a whole.

While Bruce cooked, and I tended the fire, and Peter fished, Joe and Skip set up camp each evening.

Earlier in the trip, Peter had been the most nervous, the one always the most eager to get to the outpost at Baker Lake as soon as possible, the one always voting against holidays, the one who never dawdled, the one who saved scraps of food against the day when all our food would be gone; but now he was the most relaxed man in camp.

Peter had saved us all. He had navigated the red canoe skilfully down the same cascades that had capsized the grey and the green canoes, and now he was the one who fed us with the only fishing lure left in camp. Earlier we had teased him, now we all owed our lives to him.

After the accident, I was so nervous when I embarked in a canoe that my entire body shook with fear. Peter could not help smile a bit when he saw my hands shaking, although he never openly teased me as I had once teased him.

During the day, Peter dragged his lure behind the canoe. It surfed along the lake. One day, a large fish grabbed his lure. Now it was my turn to shake with fear, to miss the others as the green canoe disappeared out of sight over the horizon, but Peter was careful not to lose the expedition's last remaining lure upon which our lives now depended. Cautious as ever, he spent half an hour calmly bringing that mammoth fish alongside.

When we stopped in the evening, I no longer took a tent and pitched it on a distant hill, nor complained when Joe and Skip lashed our two remaining tents together close to the camp fire and placed the overturned canoes to windward to protect them from approaching blizzards, nor complained when they gathered rocks and built stone walls for added protection. [Skip and Peter had rescued the second tent. It had been wedged behind the rear seat in the green canoe and thus had not been lost in the falls.] It felt so good to be close to one another and secure.

We had all changed. We all felt the same awe, the same love, the same pride in anything we could do for others. We had not been metamorphosed into "Lord of the Flies," as William Golding would say, but rather into humble flies of the Lord. As flies of the Lord, we felt three things: pride only in what we could do for others; gratitude for the love we received in return, and awe for the frightening beauty of the creation which both fed us and killed us, a beauty so magnificent it was not just worth living for, but worth dying for.

photo credit Richard Irwin
Innuit

Chapter Twenty-Four
Innuit

All morning the symphony of color played; and in the afternoon, the fires of dawn were fanned into yet more spectacular array by the setting sun. The calm lake mirrored the sky; and, as we paddled towards the horizon, our canoes carried us into that heaven where water and sky are one. Behind us the black clouds of an approaching arctic blizzard shrouded the flaming sky.

When we turned into the narrows, where the current quickened and the colorful lake transformed itself into a tumultuous river, we were surprised to see small furry animals walking about on their hind legs.

"I think they are people," Joe said in disbelief.

As we drew closer, we saw that they were Innuit children, dressed in caribou fur and playing on the tundra. When we landed, a woman emerged from the tent, also dressed in furs. Skip Pessl walked slowly towards her while the rest of us remained by the canoes. She spoke no English and seemed very frightened. Her children began to gather around her protectively. Skip rejoined us. We crossed the narrows and set up camp on the far side.

During dinner we heard the sound of an outboard motor. Suddenly, a boat came around the bend. When he saw us, the Innuit hunter turned sharply towards shore and landed. Three of his sons and a dead caribou were in the boat with him. They were smiling broadly. We invited them to share some dehydrated carrots we had found at the abandoned survey camp a couple of weeks earlier. The carrots had been packed in a large tin can. Bruce was using the bottom of the can as a pot and the top as a spoon.

The Innuit shared with us this makeshift meal with smiles. They rubbed their bellies as if it were the best food in the world. The hunter, his cheeks bulging with unswallowed carrots, disappeared behind a rock. When he returned, he was still smiling broadly and still rubbing his belly, but his cheeks were no longer bulging with carrots. He sat down again. Dehydrated carrots had not been the first choice of the Innuit hunter, nor of the survey crew, apparently: that is why they had abandoned them. They were not our choice either, but it was all we had to offer.

Before we had finished eating, the Innuit hunter pointed to the sky. Black storm clouds had been gathering in the northwest since dawn. His sons jumped up and ran to their boat. In a moment they were gone. The Arctic seemed empty without them, and soon the blizzard was upon us.

We lay low the next day while the storm swirled snow across the tundra. In the evening, the wind calmed a little as the cold Arctic air settled over our camp.

"Is that you, George?" Skip asked.

"I thought it was you."

I poked my head out and saw the Innuit hunter.

"Tea? Canoe?" he said.

Skip and the others shortly emerged from the tents, and we greeted him with smiles, but shook our heads: we had lost all our tea the day Art Moffatt died.

"Thank you, thank you," he repeated. "Tea? Canoe?"

After a while, the five of us came to the realization that he was inviting us to tea over at his place. We picked up one of the canoes, but he placed his hand gently on the bow and pressed down. He motioned for us to follow him.

Behind some rocks on the beach, there was a wooden box with a curtain in front of it. We could hear the roar of a kerosene Primus stove. The other Innuit boys and men were standing around smiling. They had prepared for us tea and a large pot of caribou steaks. I do not know if they had been planning to join us, but when they saw how hungrily we ate, they gave all the steaks to us. Everyone was smiling and laughing. We were laughing and smiling too, because we were so happy to get the food in our bellies; and they were laughing and smiling to see us so happy.

When all the meat was gone, the hunter offered us the fatty broth still left in the pot. We shook our heads politely.

The hunter tipped the pot and offered the broth to us one more time. Still we shook our heads, but he understood the look in our eyes. Finally, he spilled a little of the fat on the ground; and we all dove for it, and drank cupful after cupful of fat, until they laughed and indicated that we were Innuit.

The hunter held up his right arm and made a motion with his wrist that was the exact replica of how a caribou's ankle moved when prancing across the rocky arctic hills. We shook our heads and held up the fingers of both hands. More than two weeks had passed since we had killed our last caribou.

Darkness settled, and we went our separate ways. We were tempted to ask them to take us down the river to Baker Lake, which still was more than a hundred miles away, and we were all but out of food: but we knew he had a family to look after, and so we embarked down the rapids the following morning.

Three days later we ate our last meal. It consisted of a can of curry powder split six ways; but the Thelon River flowed fast between bedrock banks and carried us seventy miles that day to the Hudson's Bay Post at Baker Lake. The manager of the Hudson's Bay Post offered us a cup of coffee and then hurried us onto the last float plane of the season, which was ready to take off. The date was September 24th, 1955.

photo credit George Luste
Trapper's cabin on Selwyn Lake

Chapter Twenty-Five
The Trapper

One by one, the others left Churchill. I lingered, searching for a way back into the wilderness. A grey-haired lady approached me one day. She said she was the correspondent for the *Winnipeg Free Press*. She thought there might be a story in our trip and invited me to dinner. Her husband was a retired trapper. He had had a cabin on Selwyn Lake, the last lake on the Chipman river before the Height of Land. He asked me if we had passed it. I said we had.

When I had finished telling my story, the old trapper looked at me. "I bet I know how you feel," he said with a twinkle in his eye.

I smiled at him politely, thinking him a fool. I doubted very much that anyone knew how I felt: my experiences were so very personal, so uniquely my own.

"You feel lucky," he said.

photo credit David Zizzo

Laurie

Chapter Twenty-Six
The Longer Journey

When I returned home, I became the stage manager of a play that all the critics agreed was perfectly terrible; its run lasted only one night. George Segal and Peter Falk, the stars, went on to better things; I went on a bicycle trip.

I met Zaidee and her mother and brother in Seville for Holy Week, after which I toured with them for a while with my bicycle on top of their car, until the pains in my stomach grew so bad that I felt I had to escape. I got on my bicycle, went off by myself, and slept in a cave in the mountains of Spain. My ulcer perforated my intestine that night, and I lost a lot of blood, which made me feel relaxed: and I passed out.

In the Middle Ages, monks were bled once a month. The loss of blood has a calming effect on the nerves. It has the same effect as tranquilizers, except that tranquilizers add chemicals to the blood stream, while bleeding removes them; bleeding is cheaper and less damaging to the health. The next morning, I coasted dizzily down the mountain: and after convalescing in Malaga for a time, where my mother was then living, I boarded a boat home.

For four years, I holed up in a $27 a month tenement and failed four times to tell Art's story in such a way that any intelligent publisher would be interested in bring the book out.

I met Nancy Bigelow at a friend's wedding. We bought a tandem bicycle and a kayak, travelled all over the map, and married. No man was ever happier than I was. After we were married, she became pregnant, and my happiness reached new heights of ecstasy.

I decided to get serious about life. Following G.B. Shaw's advice ("Those who can, do; those who can't, teach"), I returned to school, worked like a dog, and won a fellowship in 1962 to get my Ph.D. in the History of Science at Berkeley.

A son (George Landon Grinnell) was born. My happiness reached unbelievable heights. I adored him. At Berkeley, I worked even harder, bent over double in pain with ulcers: I nearly bled to death a second time, got up, passed my exams, then collapsed with a nervous breakdown. I was finding it difficult to reconcile what I had learned from Art with what was being taught at Berkeley.

Other students at the University of California at Berkeley were rebelling, but I was not — not outwardly anyway, I just wanted to feed my young family. These were the years (1962-1967) when Mario Savio was mounting the steps of the Administration Building to denounce "The System," when students were occupying the offices of the President of the

University, when the United States Government under President Johnson was drafting the poor out of the slums of Chicago into the Army in order to defoliate Viet Nam, and when the Chancellor of the University joined me in the hospital.

I had come to Berkeley to study the history of science in general, and the history of physics in particular. I admired Werner Heisenberg, the German physicist who had placed morality above Empire and sabotaged the Nazi atom bomb project. He deliberately built the most ineffectual nuclear reactor possible, one that couldn't ever hope to reach a rolling boil, let alone critical mass.

The more I studied Heisenberg's *Physics and Philosophy*, the more I admired him. He held to the Platonic, rather than to the Kantian notion of the "rational soul." According to Plato, we humans are not just able to destroy nature with our technology, we are also able to climb the spiritual ladder to see more clearly the World from the divine perspective, a place in the soul out of which springs moral actions.

Heisenberg was not alone. Ernst Mach, Gregor Mendel, Johann Kepler, Euclid, and other great scientists had also been able to see the World from this divine perspective: but the dominant paradigm of science during the last five hundred years has developed in the opposite direction. Following the German philosopher Immanuel Kant, it has linked science with technology for the purpose of controlling, dominating, and "developing" the wilderness, with an eye to "improving" it. This "improvement" consists of spraying herbicides, insecticides and pesticides over part of the Creation, and paving over the rest with a parking lot.

In stark contrast to Heisenberg stood James Conant, the biochemist who had worked for the United States Army during the First World War in poison gas research, who had then directed the development of the atom bomb during the Second World War, and who had finished as President of Harvard University during my brief sojurn there. As President of Harvard, he had replaced all the traditional courses in the Freshman and Sophomore years with "General Education" courses, whose purpose was to indoctrinate the future leaders of the American Empire with the benefits of Manhattan-Project style science, science linked to military engineering with an endless supply of government money. This linkage of science with engineering by government money became Conant's model for winning the Cold War and improving the World. It had proved a winning combination in destroying the Germans and Japanese during the Second World War; now, he argued, we should make war on Nature in order to eliminate poverty, hunger and disease, and thereby counteract the propaganda of the Soviet Union.

The way to eliminate hunger, Conant argued, was to spray the natural world with "pesticides." Pesticides had been developed during the First World War in the form of poison gas. The "pests" then had been the enemy troops. The new pests were mosquitoes, fire ants, midges, grasshoppers.... By 1962, the year I arrived at Berkeley, Rachel Carson had pointed out in her insightful book *Silent Spring* that the birds were no longer singing in her back yard. She was dying of cancer and so was the wildlife.

In addition to producing enough food for the world by spraying our animal and plant competitors with derivatives of poison gas, Conant believed that the way to eliminate disease was to dose everyone with antibiotics and tranquilizers: antibiotics for the sick, tranquilizers for the insane.

Fifty years later, whole families of bacteria have developed immunity to the antibiotics, while we humans have lost our immunity to the bacteria. Medical bills are now driving both individuals and Governments of the Western World into a morass of debt, and the tranquilizers are not helping.

Despite spending 25 billion dollars to make "war on cancer," deaths by cancer are up 7% per hundred thousand population. In order to help patients cope with the rising cancer rate, doctors prescribed Valium until they discovered that Valium makes the tumors grow faster; and then, remember, there was Thalidomide....

Despite the lies the drug companies tell, all this money spent on medicine has not increased human longevity. Scientists in ancient Greece in the 4th Century B.C. lived an average 73.2 years. Today the average scientist lives 73.8 years, six months longer, it would seem: but on closer examination, it is not so much that scientists actually live six months longer, as that, today, they (and the rest of us) take six months longer to die, strapped to hospital beds with tubes up various orifices — for which pleasures our families pay more than a thousand dollars a day until the money runs out, and then the government goes into debt on our behalf. Ninety percent of all hospital expenses are accrued during the last six months of a person's life. In ancient Greece, "nature was its own best cure." It was at least cheaper.

In addition to making war on hunger, and war on disease, James Conant also wanted to make war on poverty through the "peaceful" development of nuclear reactors. Nuclear reactors were developed during the Second World War in order to turn uranium 238 into plutonium 239 as fuel for the mass production of nuclear weapons. In the process of producing plutonium, nuclear reactors become hot. The obvious way to carry off this heat is to connect nuclear reactors to generating stations where the heat is used in turbines to produce electricity. During the Cold War, the United States was in a nuclear bomb race with China and the Soviet Union. In order to mass-produce these nuclear weapons, it needed to mass-produce plutonium; and so nuclear bomb factories were built all over America under the guise of electrical generating stations. The heat for these reactors went to produce electricity for the gadgets of modern civilization, while the plutonium went to the atom bomb assembly plants to terrorize the world.

While America built the most powerful nuclear arsenal in the world, American garbage dumps filled up on yesterday's gadgets; and the poor ended up in the East Bronx.

When I had arrived at Berkeley, I had hoped to study under Professor Thomas S. Kuhn. Kuhn had been a graduate student in Physics at Harvard when James Conant offered him a job teaching the history of science in the new courses Conant was setting up to extol the benefits of the Manhattan-Project approach to the problems of the World. For this enterprise, Conant needed people to tell a lot of lies about the history of science, and Kuhn had been recruited; but Conant's version of history had considerable problems, and Kuhn was too honest a scholar to buy the whole propaganda package.

Conant wanted Kuhn to rewrite history so as to prove that the world had made progress since ancient times. Kuhn seemed a good prospect for the job because, as a physicist, he knew no history. The initial "assignment" Conant gave him was to teach the Galileo case. Kuhn discovered, when he researched this assignment, that Galileo and Saint Robert Bellarmine, the Grand Inquisitor, had different ways of viewing Truth. Kuhn called these different world views "paradigms" and questioned whether scientists were really able to determine which version of the truth is correct.

The hard fact is that we humans cannot survive without our technology. If we abandoned our technology and went back to hunting and fishing with stone tools, at least 99% of the human population would starve within six months. On the other hand, if we use technology unrestrained by appreciation for the gifts of the Creation, we will destroy the delicate balance of Gaia which provides us with the air we breathe, the warmth we feel, the water we drink, and the food we eat. To achieve some sort of balance, the power of science and technology over nature needs to be restrained by morality.

When I arrived at Berkeley in the autumn of 1962, Kuhn was on leave in Europe interviewing Werner Heisenberg, Niels Bohr and the other founders of quantum physics; and so I was not able to study with him that year. I found myself instead in a seminar under Professor John C. Greene, who had recently published a book called *The Death of Adam*.

Like Kuhn, Greene had been a graduate student at Harvard when Conant was President there. Like Kuhn, he had been dragooned into seeing the world from Conant's perspective; and like Kuhn, he had difficulty rewriting history to conform to Conant's Manhattan-Project approach to the improvement of Nature.

John C. Greene's book was about the replacement of the Christian with the Evolutionary World View. Greene maintained a neutral stance in class, as did Kuhn; but beneath the surface, it was clear that he was more sympathetic with the Christian World View than he ought to have been if he expected to flourish on that Academic stage. He was "let go" the following year, but not before planting a seed in my brain that the stories I had been told about Charles Darwin, the founder of modern evolutionary theories, were not exactly true: and I soon found myself in another unresolvable dilemma. If I wanted to get and hold a job, I was going to have to learn to tell a lot of Conant-type lies about some of the heroes of modern science: and so I retired to a hospital bed and stared at the walls for forty days.

In 1832, Charles Darwin had sailed around the world on a warship of the British Royal Navy, H.M.S. Beagle. Darwin had helped raise the British flag on the Falkland Islands, had ridden with the Gauchos under General Rosas in their war of extermination against the Arachanians, and had danced in celebration on the graves of the native Tasmanians.

After four years travelling around the globe, Darwin had been happy to arrive in Tasmania. The Island reminded him of England and there was much dancing and singing by settlers to welcome the arrival of H.M.S. Beagle: but the Captain of the Beagle, Robert Fitzroy, did not dance and sing. He felt that dancing on the graves of the natives was not in accord with the teachings of Christ, and he persuaded Darwin to help him write a defence of the work of the missionaries. Darwin obliged, but his heart was elsewhere. After another year of Imperial tourism, Darwin repudiated Christian morality in favor of the long-discarded doctrine of "survival of the fittest."

About two thousand years ago, Epicurus and his followers had exchanged the gods of morality for the goddess of sexuality, Venus. Through the fecundity of sex, the "fittest" had survived in a competitive world: and this was good, they had argued. Lucretius, the most elegant spokesman for Epicureanism, had been writing during the most destructive phase of the Roman Empire, when slaves and wealth from around the Mediterranean were pouring into Rome; but soon the Roman generals and bankers took to fighting among themselves, and when the dust had cleared, Stoicism emerged victorious, then Platonism, and finally Christianity. The Fathers of the Church replaced the Epicurean ideal of "survival of the fittest" with the beatitudes of Christ: "blessed are the meek for they shall inherit the Earth" — at least, so they hoped.

In 1803, British settlers had landed in Tasmania and had gone on "hunts" until, by 1833, about twenty thousand native Tasmanians had been killed off and their land filched. The surviving 120 Tasmanians were rescued by a missionary and carried off to Flinders Island; none survive, and thus the Tasmanian race has fallen into extinction.

In the end, Darwin found the Tasmanian episode inspiring. Like other British Imperialists, he believed that the annihilation of the Tasmanians and other "darker races" was a dandy way to improve the human species: and, in 1859, he published his famous (or infamous) book: *On the Origin of Species by means of Natural Selection, or the Preservation of Favoured Races in the Struggle for Life*, based on this Tasmanian example. Later (in 1871) he expanded his ideas in the *Descent of Man*. In between the publication of these two books, he set back the science of genetics about two thousand years with his erroneous theories of blending inheritance, the inheritance of acquired characters, and pangenesis.

In his *Descent of Man*, Darwin divided the world between "superior" and "inferior" races. The white races he believed to be superior and the "darker races" inferior. In order to improve the species, Darwin argues, it is necessary, if "in some ways regrettable," to cull out the Tasmanians and other darker races.

He also argued that it was necessary to cull out the Irish, who, although white, were clearly degenerate because they were Catholic. Darwin contended that "the best minds" had gone into the Church during the middle ages and had been forced to take vows of celibacy. This had lowered the I.Q. of the human race, which was why it was the Englishman's duty not just to eliminate the darker races, but Roman Catholics as well. Accordingly, Darwin encouraged British landlords to ship food out of Catholic Ireland into Protestant England. This practice led to the decline of the Irish population from eight down to three million, while the English population increased from eight up to forty million during the same period.

In order to dress up British racism as "scientific fact," Darwin spent forty-five years distorting data, inventing false theories, and telling lies, which is why fascists, imperialists and free enterprise capitalists have all celebrated him so much — and why anyone who now dares to criticize Darwin is not allowed to teach in American schools.

Basically Darwin's "scientific" argument is this: what the British settlers did in Tasmania was "natural" because it was no different from what British animal breeders were doing back in England. What animal breeders were doing back in England was importing Merino sheep from Spain to breed with

British sheep, because the wool of Merino sheep is softer that British wool. They imported stallions from Arabia to breed with British mares, to improve the stamina of British horses; and they imported pigs from China to breed with British pigs, because Chinese pigs had shorter legs, and thus did not waste so much energy running around as did British pigs. After the cross-breeding took place, British breeders selected pigs with the shorter legs, the more vigorous stallions, and sheep with the softer wool. They culled out the inferior British throw-backs and thereby introduced new "genes" (or what were called "factors" then) into the British animal population. Darwin saw this culling out of inferior stock as similar to what the British settlers had done in Tasmania, and thus claimed there was a link between the race wars of the British Empire and domestic animal breeding.

However, the flaw in the argument was that the British settlers had not shipped Tasmanian males back to England to breed with the ladies of the British aristocracy; they had simply "culled" them out. To get around this obvious lapse in the analogy, Darwin proposed three erroneous theories of inheritance: blending inheritance, the inheritance of acquired characters, and pangenesis.

Although Gregor Mendel, a Catholic monk, corrected Darwin's errors in 1865, Darwin published his *Variations of Animals and Plants under Domestication* three years later, in order to successfully bury Mendel's corrections. Darwin's two volumes are a distortion of ten thousand years of domestic plant and animal breeding and a complete fabrication: but lies are the food of Empire, and so Mendel's paper was repressed for 32 years while Darwin, for his contribution to racism, for his justification of the atrocities of the British Empire, and for his corruption of science, was buried with honor in Westminster Abbey — and today is held up as the paragon of scientific probity in American schools.

If Darwin's first error was an attempted analogy between British imperial warfare and British animal breeding, his second error was an attempted analogy between "artificial" and "natural" selection. According to Darwin's theory, population pressure in Nature, as in England, resulted in "survival of the fittest." Weaker individuals did not survive and thereby English businessmen and other animals had found themselves much improved. This form of "natural selection," he argued, was similar to the "artificial selection" of the animal breeders, which in turn was analagous to the extermination of the Tasmanians. All were "natural," by analogy; but none of his analogies stand up to scrutiny.

In the wilderness, wolves do not "improve" the caribou by selectively eating them. If they did, the surviving "improved" caribou would soon be able to outrun the wolves, thereby driving the wolves into extinction. Nature does not select "superior" races nor "superior" individuals; it selects beautiful, interdependent, ecological systems. Moss, caribou and wolves are linked together in a miraculous web that needs no improvement, not by us, not by God, not even by Martians. Even if wolves converted to

Buddhism and gave up meat-eating, it would not improve the ecological balance. Their teeth are designed to tear flesh, not grind grain, so they would soon become extinct; and, without wolves to cull out the old and the ill, the caribou would overgraze the tundra, and the whole ecological system fall apart. But Empires are built on different principles.

Although wolves, caribou and moss are linked together in a beautiful web of interdependence, we imperialists do not starve when we drive Aurochs into extinction (1627), nor Tasmanians (1878) nor Quaggas (1883), nor Pig-footed Bandicoots (1907); we simply replace them, along with other extinct species, with our domesticated plants, cattle, horses and pigs — and we shovel grain into our domestic animals in feed lots. In nature, selection operates for the preservation of the whole Creation. In Empires, selection operates for the benefit of the winning race at the expense of the whole Creation.

I was brought up to believe in Darwinian theories of race warfare as a means of "improving" the species. My great grandfather, General Ernst, was not just Chief Engineer for the United States Army, but the commanding officer at West Point and thus Chief Racist there. I have inherited his library. Young West Point officers, under my great grandfather's tutelage, went out West to slaughter the bison and the Cheyenne by way of improving America.

And so, as a graduate student at Berkeley in 1963, I lay in a hospital bed and stared at the walls.

One afternoon, a lady from the Episcopal Church popped her head around the door. She looked into my insane eyes and apologized for the intrusion. I did not reply, and she left; but I began to get the idea that if I could survive until Easter, I might recover my sanity. On Easter Sunday, I crawled out of my hospital bed to her Church and felt at peace once again.

Hard working, a judicious kisser of ass, and mentally unstable, I had the basic qualifications for a Ph.D. I completed my dissertation on Darwin in such an incomprehensible manner that it eventually passed. No one detected what heresies lay beneath its pedantic surface, except Professor Hunter Dupree, another product of Conant's Harvard: he called the study "sophomoric" and resigned as Chairman of the committee in protest. When I was offered a job at McMaster University, I fled to Canada hastily.

I loved my wife and son above all things. I was grateful for the caribou who had died for me, and grateful for the Christian, Buddhist, and other mystics who have walked softly on the Earth to redeem the sins of my humanity: but, above all, I was grateful for my job. No lie was too big or too small for me to tell to keep it.

Nancy, my wife, was wonderful, self-sacrificing, heroic: and she wished she had married someone else. As a professor, I was clearly a great genius, correct in all my pronouncements. Every time she tried to talk to me, I graced her with a fifty minute lecture. Grateful as she was for such edification, she nonetheless became depressed and seemed to want me out of the house: or at least I thought she wanted me out of the house. Perhaps she just wanted me to tell the truth, or talk to her as if we were both human beings.

We parted company. Our eldest son went on drugs: and when he was eighteen, I received a call from Nancy (now happily remarried in Washington D.C. to a nice Colonel in the American Air Force in charge of weapons procurement for the Pentagon) telling me that Georgie had freaked out. I flew down to pick him up. Sylvia, my second wife, and I took Georgie on a hike on Good Friday, and he babbled on for three days. On Easter morning, he stopped babbling and fell into a deep sleep; and when he woke up, he was at peace with himself once more. He returned to Washington to complete his final year in high school, took more drugs, freaked out again, and this time was placed in a mental hospital for forty days down in Washington. I moved down to Washington and visited him every day. When again he recovered, he returned with me to Canada, went back on drugs and freaked out a third time. The psychiatrist said he was schizophrenic and should be institutionalized for the rest of his life.

Sylvia and I visited him every day: but one day, he was not at the hospital. He had decided to walk home. It was a fifteen mile hike. That summer, I packed him and our other two sons, Chuck and Andrew, into a rowboat, and we headed down the Saint Lawrence River. We rowed the length of Lake Ontario, rowed through the Thousand Islands. Rowed down the abandoned Gulop, Soulange and

Racine Canals, rowed through downtown Montreal, rowed passed Quebec City and headed out to sea.

By the time we had reached Kingston, Georgie was off drugs and onto booze. By the time we had reached Trois Riviere, he preferred a good steak to drugs or booze. After forty days on the Saint Lawrence River, we were out to sea, and Georgie was once again his old self and at peace.

Unable to find a job in Canada, Georgie rode his bicycle down to Washington D.C. to join the U.S. Marines. He met Betty Emer on the way. She had earned enough money working nights at a Seven-Eleven store to buy a tent, a sleeping bag, and a bicycle, but not enough money to rent an apartment: so she mounted her bicycle and rode west. Never mind the Marines, Georgie turned around and headed west with her.

They crossed Canada to the Pacific, turned south to Mexico, turned east to Florida, turned north to home. By the time they had returned from their 17,000 mile Odyssey, our second son, Nathaniel, had taken George's place in the Marines; and our third son had followed George into drugs, had dropped out of High School and was living with friends off the Canadian Saving Bonds I had put in his name to pay for his college education.

George tracked Andrew down and volunteered to take him on a forty day trip into the wilderness as an alternative to drugs. I drove Andrew, George, Betty and Sandy to Sioux Lookout, where they embarked down the Albany River in Art Moffatt's footsteps.

My nephew, Alexander ("Sandy") Host, had been taking his Ph.D. in environmental science at Rutgers:

and he had suffered, like me, a nervous breakdown, and so the four of them embarked down the longest wilderness river in Northern Ontario in quest of that elusive inner peace. Forty days later, they had reached FortAlbany safely. They called home, happy and at peace.

Art used to get on a boat at Fort Albany, which had taken him and his companions down the dangerous James Bay coast to the railhead at Moosenee: but the boat was no longer running, so on July 18th, 1984, Georgie, Betty, Sandy and Andy caught the outgoing tide and turned south along the coast of James Bay towards Moosenee.

[August 8th, 1984, *The Spectator*]: The official search for four canoeists missing on the barren James Bay coast was called off last night.

But aircraft making regular flights in the area will continue to watch the coast for any new signs of the missing people.

"As long as there is the slightest ray of hope, we'll continue to look," Sergeant Peter Hamilton of the OPP Moosonee detachment said this morning. He added, however, that the chances of finding them "diminish day by day."

An OPP Otter aircraft out of South Porcupine conducted its final intensive aerial search yesterday, said Sgt. Hamilton, but it will "continue observation while on its regular flights up and down the coast."

The search will continue through Friday in a reduced form as three police and Ontario Natural Resources Ministry aircraft and private aircraft owned by Bushland Airways, "as part of their regular flights," patrol the west coast of James Bay and Hannah Bay in the southern end of James Bay, he said. On Friday the situation will be assessed, and will likely continue until the people have been found.

Those flights will watch for any sign of the four paddlers who haven't been seen since July 18 when they left Fort Albany for Moosenee. The search started August 1 after an American relative contacted police to say they were overdue.

Missing are Andrew Grinnell, 16, and his brother George, 22, both of Lynden, their cousin Alexander Host, 30, of Old Greenwich, Conn., and Betty Emer, 23 of Cresskill, N.J.

Four days after they left Fort Albany the area was hit by a bad storm, which grounded OPP aircraft for four days, Sgt. Hamilton said.

On Saturday, the search team found a running shoe, a cooler, two foam pads, a tent and a backpack containing Andrew's wallet. Also discovered were two abandoned canoes, which dimmed hopes of finding the foursome alive. Two life jackets that may have belonged to the group were also found.

A rope had been tied to the stern seat of the canoe Sandy and Andy were in. The other end of the rope had been tied to the bow seat of the canoe Betty and Georgie were in. The rope had broken. Andy's body was never found. May God have mercy on them all and also on me.

After they died, Sylvia took me hiking in the Arctic. She took me kayaking in the lower Saint Lawrence. She walked me across England, walked me across France. She walked me up the Alps to Chamonix. She did everything she could to bring me back. She is a wonderful woman and I am eternally grateful to her, but I was despondent and only wanted to escape this world. I did not know where I wanted to escape to. I just wanted to escape, escape from my job, from people, most of all I wanted to escape from God.

Sylvia, Dr. Sylvia Bowerbank, was not an escapist. Published scholar, award-winning teacher, rising force in the feminist movement, at work on a major treatise on "landscape and literature," she was not ready to walk away from life: and for five years, she would not let me walk away either, and so I paced back and forth in front of students at McMaster University, where I had taught for twenty-four years.

In class one day, Laurie, a student, wrote a poem about me called "The Lecturer":

Seconds screamed loudly
Where there were no words
And up against a wall
He would pace out terror
And then begin.
He would lay his thoughts
On the platform of words
Carefully, cautiously, one eye
On the clock to measure the space
Where Hell lay, and where one must recant
The words of Angels.

Half admiration
For those who didn't care —
And contempt, really, for those who did.
Faces were perspectives
Where one tried universes
And maintained the God
Of art and poetry and hopeless science.
Each step measured out anger,
And fevered isolation, and disregard.
Framing the question
Almost as an afterthought —
The anguished attempt to catch a harmony
One has once heard —
Eyes were wild gesticulations,
And humaneness lay buried
Beneath outright fear.

A pause would recline silently
Blinking back from a yawning gap.

And what did this have to do anyway
With the deaths of sons
And all those painful living minds
Could not account for the two that were
stilled
And silent, endlessly silent,
And the quiet of a stone
Where a life once was.
Sanctuary was not here.

Six years after their death, I walked. I walked
away from Sylvia, walked away from my job, walked
away from life; but before I died, I wanted to do one

more thing, I wanted to tell Art's story. I had been trying to tell it for more than thirty years without success. I had turned to others for help, and they had helped; mostly they had helped me correct my punctuation.

One day after she had graduated, Laurie stopped into my office to tell me she had been accepted at Teacher's College. I turned to her for help and handed her my manuscript. After a couple of weeks, she handed it back without the punctuation corrected. She only said, "Tell the truth." And so now, forty years later, I have written the story again. I hope I have told the truth.

As the Buddhists say: Enlightenment is like a fountain, the pure waters well up from the earth and sparkle in the sun, then fall back to the earth to form mud. And out of the mud, the wildflowers bloom.

> In a room where there were faces in frames,
> Continuations, God, and Music
> Children were again born,
> And fatherhood stirred
> Against the questions, and the presence,
> Part of the Lecturer drown
> Washed up against the quiet of stone,
> And the aliveness of Earth.
>
>   - Laurie

And now, forty-two years after my father died, forty years after Art died, and eleven years after Sandy and Andy, Georgie and Betty died, I look into

Laurie's eyes and into the eyes of our daughter, Bethany, and once again I feel the grace of God.

photo credit George Luste
Arriving Home

COMMENTARY

Thoughts on the Moffatt Tragedy, Wilderness Canoeing, and Safety

George J. Luste

"We must. We must beware of the cold water," I repeated to myself over and over again, like a mantra, after reading the *Sports Illustrated* article that described Arthur Moffatt's death. That was in early 1969, the same year I was to canoe down the Dubawnt River, where he had died fourteen years earlier.

I survived my trip safely, and in part I feel obligated to Art Moffatt for that being the case. His death caused me to pause, to reflect, and so to take precautions which otherwise I might not have done before my initial trip into the Barrens in 1969. Since then I have gone back ten more times to the Northwest Territories for extended pilgrimages into a wilderness that Art saw for the first time the last

279

summer of his life. In this regard I have been very "lucky".

The author of this book has asked me to try and share with you some of my thoughts and attitudes about wilderness canoeing, based on my own experiences. I feel privileged to do so in this book. If my words lead to some pause and reflection on the part of the reader, if they make one wilderness trip a bit safer, my purpose will be realized.

———————————————

Arthur Moffatt died on a northern canoe trip. So did George Grinnell's two teenage sons. So have others.

Is northern canoeing really as dangerous as these tragedies would seem to suggest? I don't believe so. That is not to say there are no risks in canoeing. There are risks in everything we do. It's all relative. By way of comparison, driving an automobile for a day on a busy expressway in the rain frightens me far more today than paddling 500 miles for four weeks in the northern wilderness.

Both of the above canoe accidents, on the Dubawnt and on James Bay, had significant common elements. Both involved cold water, both involved swamping, and both involved a sudden extreme situation that one was not able to cope with. The victims faced situations that were totally new, situations with which they had no prior experience. There were no gradual warnings. Both were cataclysmic and unforgiving, almost hopeless as they occurred.

The *Sports Illustrated* article focused my thoughts so that even I could see the obvious—that prolonged cold water immersion would be our greatest danger in the Barrens and must be avoided at all costs. To help avoid a similar catastrophe I made a very primitive nylon decking for part of my canoe for the 1969 trip, to keep it from swamping immediately in a similar accident. It was a crude affair and only partially effective. My thought at the time was that all I needed was a second chance to survive a mistake in a rapid. Today I never travel in the far north without a much improved and very substantial waterproof snap-on canoe cover, one that lets waves wash completely over the decking.

It is possible that a similar canoe cover might have prevented both tragedies. But my conjecture, well after the fact, is not meant to admonish. Knowing what is the best course of action, before one has experience, is often impossible. The history of travel in the north is replete with stories where inexperienced individuals almost perished on their first journey, but returned a second or a third time, and with the lessons learned, avoided many prior mistakes. John Franklin came within a whisker of dying on his first arctic venture but had a relatively easy go the second time. Likewise J.B. Tyrrell, in

1893, on the Dubawnt trip, he suffered terribly and collapsed from cold and starvation. Yet a year later, in 1894, he had a relatively easy time on the adjoining Kazan River. My own experience was similar. On my second trip into the Barrens I travelled father, with less discomfort and less danger, than on the first trip. On my most recent traverse, a solo canoe trip across four watersheds from Chipman Lake to Arviat on Hudson Bay, I felt so relaxed and safe—it was like returning home. My main concern was that perhaps I was too relaxed, and thus at some risk because of this.

We do learn from our own mistakes, if we survive them, and can learn from those made by others. Reading travel books on the north has been a lifelong passion for me, in part, to learn from the more horrendous tales, how not to travel and what mistakes to avoid. I see no value in surviving a terrifying experience for its own sake. The value is in the journey itself, in the landscape and one's spiritual relationship with it, the fauna and flora, the solitude and the physical joy of paddling, not in enduring an unnecessary ordeal.

Besides learning from my own mistakes and those of others I have always tried to sensitize myself to the possibility of the unexpected, to remind myself not to get over-confident and not to feel like "I know it all". To illustrate, some years ago while paddling the long length of Point Lake on the Coppermine River I kept reflecting on Rocky Defile. Rocky Defile, named by John Franklin, was the next major canyon and rapids we had to deal with. I knew it had claimed at least five canoeists over several prior summers and I kept asking myself, "Why?" Surely all these people had decided it was safe enough. I could only conclude that they had all been misled by what they saw, thinking it was within their ability to paddle but realizing to the contrary too late. To my mind here was evidence that one's scouting judgment might be lacking in fully appraising the deadly nature of this body of water. There had to be factors that were not self-evident, unseen factors. Thus I decided I would carry my canoe around, no matter what. This I did, portaging the canoe on the first trip, before we even scouted the rapid.

After portaging Rocky Defile we had a leisurely lunch at the lip of the canyon to enjoy the view. Studying the water below, while we ate, I could not see how, at our low water level, there was any serious danger in paddling Rocky Defile that day. There had to be an explanation. I mused that maybe looking down at the rapid, from forty feet above it, could be misleading. So, after lunch, to fully convince myself, I decided to scale the walls in mid-canyon down to the water to have an eye level look. This I did and the water did look runable. The irony was that the climb down and then back up was probably more dangerous than running the rapid would have been. Therein lies the serendipity of human rationality or something like that.

This leads to another observation. Water levels can vary tremendously and are crucial in determining risk. At one level, sometimes higher but more often lower, a rapid or a river may be runable but at another water level it may be suicidal. The lesson is, don't take somebody else's word based on a trip last summer about an "easy" rapid. Relying totally on any description of a river is not recommended. Art Moffatt, following Tyrrell's notes, was not expecting the rapid in which he swamped and then died.

Maps can also be misleading. Don't assume the topographical map from the government is always correct. You could easily encounter a drop that wasn't noted on the map. Some days the wind will carry the sound of a rapid to you before you see it. Other days it may do the opposite. There is no substitute for direct visual observation, tempered with alertness and caution at all times on a river.

A phrase that I heard years ago and which I try to subscribe to is: "If you aren't willing to swim a rapid, don't consider running it." I say try to subscribe to because there are times that even with some element of risk, one may choose to run and not portage. But the evaluation of the risk should be realistic and accurate.

Even though a rapid looks easy, the coldness of the water makes a critical difference in evaluating its risk. This cannot be overstated. A dump that in a southern climate is easily survived and is part of the fun, can, in cold arctic waters, become deadly. At times when judging rapids in the arctic one tends to forget how cold the water really is, in particular if one is dry and comfortably warm while standing on shore and doing the scouting. For years I used to purposely travel with canvas sneakers on my feet. They were invariably wet and so my feet were icy cold most of the day. In this self-inflicted state of cold misery one is far less inclined towards heroics when scouting a rapid than when shrouded in a warm outfit and a false sense of security.

Air temperature also effects risk. A cold water dump in the Barrens that may be survivable, or even refreshing, on a warm sunny day in July can become hypothermic on a cold and windy day in September. Wet cold is miserable in particular in the arctic beyond the treeline, where one cannot build robust warming fires. I think that perhaps the cold wet days of fall in the north are the most dangerous as far as exposure and hypothermia go. I have found it is far easier to be comfortable at -40 in the middle of winter than at zero in the fall on a soggy and wet day with a breeze. While paddling, the physical exertion usually keeps one reasonably warm, even if damp or wet. The cold and shivering set in when you stop paddling.

Proper clothing and equipment are important for both comfort in normal circumstances and for survival in emergencies. There are numerous outdoor books which dwell on this in detail and we shall not do so here. The Moffatt party was not well equipped by today's standards, even taking into account that 1955 was the pre-Royalex and pre-Gortex era.

Were the cold water and September air temperature the only contributing factors towards Art's death? I don't believe so. Surely other factors came into play, such as the group's physical and mental condition at the time of the dump.

The accident occurred two-and-a-half months into their trip. In reading George's account, it is evident that not enough food, or more specifically, food with high caloric value, such as fat, was purchased for the trip. This long, on short food rations, would have consumed much, if not all, of the body fat their bodies had started with. On my Dubawnt trip, in half the time (five weeks), I lost about 20 pounds and was much more vulnerable to the cold than at the start of the trip. That was another lesson I learned. "Better 50 lbs too much food than 5 lbs too little food," became a motto of my future trips. Carrying the excess food is hard work on the portages but there is the payback feeling of security that goes with having more food in your bowl at the end of the day than you want to eat. The most I have ever carried in my canoes is seven weeks of food, That is quite a load. At about 2.5 pounds per person per day, that totals to 245 pounds per canoe. I don't think one can carry food for three months. Today, on a long trip, like the Moffatt trip, one should arrange for a food drop-off or fly-in midway into the trip.

Cold and starvation are recurring themes in early arctic travels. In 1893, Joseph Burr Tyrrell, together with his brother James, traversed and explored without maps, the Barrens via the Dubawnt River. This was exactly the same route the Moffatt party travelled. They were the first white people to do so, together with native guides. They too ran short of provisions and nearly perished from cold and hunger before they barely made it to Churchill on Hudson Bay on October 19th. Later J. B. claimed that there are only two essentials in life—food and warmth. In his own wry way he went on to say it was nice to have both, but, of the two, food was the more important.

J.B. Tyrrell, who Art Moffatt wrote to before his trip, was a remarkable man. His outlook was practical and to the point. "The purpose of life is to live," is another quote I recall. In seven words it seems to say all that is necessary.

The prophetic John Hornby described the Barren Lands as the "land of feast and famine". It was his intention to write a book with that title but ironically enough famine found him first. Winter caught him in the middle of the Barrens, on the Thelon River, with insufficient food; famine followed and he starved to death on April 16th, 1927. His two younger companions died soon after. His story has become part of the legend of the sub-arctic landscape.

The Moffatt party was woefully short of provisions and caloric energy sustenance, they travelled very slowly and of course the cold, uncompromising reality of approaching winter and frigid water was their eventual master. On August 14 Moffatt wrote in his diary: "Most conversation revolves around food." It would be another six weeks before the survivors reached Baker Lake. Food became their all consuming pre-occupation, not only during the day and at meals, but even at night in their dreams. I cannot be certain but I do think that perhaps their ordeal during and after the dump would have been easier if each had had twenty more pounds of body fat to insulate them and sustain their body furnace. But I am not a medical doctor and cannot justify such a claim with a physiological argument.

To speculate on their mental state and its effect on survival is even more problematic. Yet it is a fact that Art died and the others survived. The question that comes to my mind is: "Is the reason Art died due only to physical exposure, or is part of the reason mental?" "Was Art's will to live diminished in any way relative to his younger companions?" I think perhaps so, for several reasons. The impression one has is that Art could not reconcile his yearning for the simple life of the wilderness with his responsibilities and financial obligations back home. Prospects for his wilderness movie did not look promising, even by September. His stubborn hold on the camera chest during the dump would suggest something akin to that. His languishing reluctance to travel faster suggest to me a form of procrastination, perhaps an indication that he was reluctant to return to civilization, back to a life that went against his instincts and longings.

The will to live can be an important factor. Years ago I read Lindeman's incredible tale of his solo kayak crossing of the Atlantic. In preparing for the ocean ordeal he put considerable effort into preparing his state of mind. He repeated "I shall make it," over and over again to himself for months until it was deeply imprinted in his psyche. He felt it was critical in surviving, in particular when he became delirious.

The second speculative conjecture I have is that as Art lay on the beach, wet and cold, and half unconscious, he was terrified that, while he was helpless himself, some of the others might die. He was the organizer of the trip, the oldest, the "leader" and the prospect of explaining the death of one of the "youngsters" to a parent was too horrible to contemplate. Such anxiety could not be conducive for a focused will to live. The others, all much younger, would not be burdened with this sense of responsibility in the same way during the survival ordeal after the dump.

Similar anticipations or fears of responsibility have visited me during trips. To illustrate, on three occasions I have canoed the northernmost coast of Labrador, where one is exposed to the crossing of wide big bays and fiords and in places must paddle along vertical cliffs for a shoreline. During such paddles one realizes how exposed and vulnerable to the elements one really is, that the winds could come up and turn a chop into a nightmare maelstrom. What would I do in a hypothetical scenario where the other canoe turned over and I could barely stay upright myself in the storm? Would I make an effort to help the other canoe in a desperate, hopeless situation, when I knew it was totally futile, or should I try and save myself? I pray that I will never have to face such a choice. This is one reason why a trip with a single canoe is more relaxing for me. With only one canoe and one paddler, the possibility of one surviving and others perishing does not exist.

The Moffatt party travelled very slowly, at least by today's canoe trip standards. But they had no preconceived standards, they were charting new ground. The long wilderness pilgrimage to the far north was not common then. It was a unique excursion, and by the end of August their group was more in tune with John Hornby's carefree travels of the past than with my own more disciplined approach of today. In a way I envy them. By comparison, my own trips north seem too brief and probably carry more of my urban mindset and habits than is necessary.

My northern trips are taken during my annual vacations. My reward comes from the moments of spiritual communion with the landscape and a sense of my existence in it. This is what I yearn for and I have no commercial objectives. Arthur Moffatt, on the other hand, was burdened with a need to realize some financial return with his film. He needed to succeed in some way with it in order to support his family. (I am reminded that in 1903 Leonidas Hubbard died in Labrador while seeking a similar commercial goal to his exploratory enterprise.) This lends a totally different cast to the Moffatt trip compared to that of the modern recreational canoeist.

However I don't get the sense that they realized that their margin of safety was diminishing as summer left them in August and chilly air temperatures, cold rain and finally snow were becoming the norm. They were not equipped for fall and early winter canoeing in the north. Why then were they still on the river in mid-September far from Baker Lake, behind Tyrrell's schedule in 1893, and with full knowledge how brief the arctic summer is? After mid-August the weather can become dicey in the Barrens. Why did they linger so?

I don't think I really know the answer, or even if there is an answer. By September they were enjoying themselves in a seemingly languid fashion. George was exploring a welcoming new reality and almost oblivious to the cold. Art was reluctant to return to the materialistic world with a failed film project. It is more difficult to surmise what Skip, Bruce and Joe were thinking. Of the six, only Peter Frank seems to have been aware and visibly concerned. But by this phase of their trip a strange state of democratic equality had been established in the group of six—

and of course, like all good committees, when everybody "assumes" responsibility, nobody really does. Instead, alliances and attitudes prevail, not common sense. I believe that this was a contributing factor to the course of events.

Mountaineering people talk of a "group mentality", by which the individuals tend to abdicate individual responsibility for their decisions because of the presence and reassurance of the group. The group provides an illusory sense of comfort and safety. The presence of the others must have, in an unthinking way reassured each individual in the Moffatt party that things were fine, thereby providing a false sense of security to each individual. Peter Franck was the exception, the practical realist. But like a knowing victim in a Shakespearean tragedy, even though he saw the problem, he lacked the personality and will to affect events.

For many years I used to think that two canoes, with four people was the ideal size for long, efficient, and safe canoe trips. It's a fact that the larger the group the slower the rate of travel. Three canoes are slower than two. And the more people, the more "social" problems that can arise. With four people and two canoes, one still has "back-up" in case one canoe gets in trouble or is lost. Yet in the Moffatt dump, all would have been lost if one of the three canoes had not survived the drop. But perhaps with a smaller group they would not have made the initial mistake.

It goes against conventional canoeing lore, but I now think that I am safer on a long canoe trip with just one canoe rather than with two. The advantages a second canoe provides in the event one canoe gets in trouble, is, I believe, often offset by the disadvantages of increased likelihood of trouble arising from the presence of the second canoe. In addition I tend to be more cautious when there is only one canoe, and there are the special rewards of a different relationship with your surroundings when you are alone.

The following quote about "alone-ness" by Henry Russell (1834-1909), the French mountaineer, comes from Elliot Merrick's *Between You and Me*.

"... although it sounds at first like an absurd paradox, I believe that a mountaineer will never acquire the quality he needs most—that is, an almost limitless confidence in himself—unless he is frequently alone in fog snow and storm in the very midst of cliffs, and dependent, with the exception of providence, solely upon himself. It has often seemed to me that in pairs people mutually frighten each other. A man is more courageous in the mountains when he is alone. It is happiness to be two, it is a lesson to be alone."

Over the years a number of unfounded versions or representations of the Moffatt accident have made their way into the canoeing literature. I've read statements like" "After some discussion there came a momentous decision. To save time the party would run any rapid which looked safe from the top." and "Everyone was rescued quickly so there should have been no problems." or "Increasing desperation made them run rapids without careful checking," or "...to speed progress they would run any rapid that looked passable from the top..." and "On Moffatt's trip, the canoeist's surviving the mid-September swamping first picked up all the packs, then the swamped members, a fatal mistake." It seems as if a liberal amount of imagination has been invoked by these writers to change the facts so they fit their preoccupations and desires for culpability.

Interpreting events is a tricky business. I suspect all of us who read this book will probably go away with a slightly different interpretation of what this trip was all about and what happened. My own view has changed considerably from when I first read the *Sports Illustrated* article in 1969 to how I see it today, in 1995, after reading this book and corresponding with the author. The truth is subjective and illusory when it comes to recollection and interpretation. Kurasawa's film *Rashomon* is a wonderful study of how illusive it can be. I suppose we can never by absolutely certain that we have it right. This comes with being honest about our own subjectivity, its limitations and its bias.

On reading the details of the fateful September 14 dump, one is struck by how close all six came to perishing in the cold water. Numerous more tragic scenarios come to mind. If the one canoe had not managed to stay afloat while going over the second drop, nobody would have survived. If Peter Frank had not had the skill (or luck) to keep the last canoe upright when George fell in, it is difficult to imagine how any of them would have survived. Touching bottom at the last moment saved George as Peter was trying to drag him to land. The lucky proximity of the island, that allowed for the rescue of Skip and Bruce, may have been critical to saving both of them. The availability of some dry sleeping bags was another critical factor. Bruce's sleeping bag, from the first pack rescued, may have made the difference between life and death for both George and Joe. The fact that Skip was physically able to keep going and together with Peter help set up camp may have been decisive in saving lives. Peter's bag of dry wood enabled them to provide some hot food. The sunshine and warmth of the following day was a godsend. The list of lucky, yet critical, factors that kept five of the six alive could probably be much longer.

In the midst of such calamities one does not have the luxury of carefully thinking through in a slow and deliberate manner what to do and when to do it. To the contrary, everything is chaotic and frantic at the time, as individuals struggle to save themselves and their colleagues. Every action can be debated after the fact. But to what purpose? Hopefully, only to sharpen one's appreciation of the risks and to learn how to cope with similar emergencies. Every situation is unique. Some may advocate "safety rules". I fear that general rules can be dangerous if they become a substitute for personal judgment.

For example, a general rule that one should rescue people in the water before rescuing packs may seem like a good rule in the abstract or in the comfort of a Toronto board room, but it may be the wrong thing to do in an emergency in the arctic. In the cold wintry conditions of September, losing your equipment can be certain death. Both Joe and Art held onto packs while in the icy water and close to losing consciousness. Supporting equipment is crucial for survival and some risk may be necessary to try and save both. One only has to read Nansen's *Farthest North* and the account of his jumping into frigid arctic waters, at great risk to his life, to swim after his empty, drifting-away kayak to realize this. Perhaps Art might have lived if Peter and George had not stopped to pick up a pack on their way to rescue him. But perhaps more would have died with him if they had not stopped to do so. The first pack Peter and George rescued, as they were paddling for Art and Joe, turned out to hold Bruce's sleeping bag, which may have saved the two lives later. The dunking of George with the second pack can be interpreted either way, as unfortunate or fortunate. Because of that dunking they realized that it would be impossible to haul anybody from the water directly into the canoe, that instead people had to be towed to shore. If they had not realized this and tried to haul somebody into the canoe, they may well have turned the last canoe over and nobody would have survived.

One can speculate and imagine a host of scenarios, of both types, less fortunate as well as more fortunate, and argue back and forth. The fact that five survived what was an extremely desperate situation seems to me to be as significant as the fact that one died.

I have never experienced anything comparable to their dump. It leaves me sober and subdued to think on it, and grateful that fate has not dealt me such a hand. We can reflect on it, and so perhaps avoid a similar tragic accident. We can try to be better prepared to deal with a similar situation. What should one do? My short list would be as follows: First, as mentioned earlier, use a water-tight snap on canoe cover when paddling in cold water. (The Inuit, who live in the Arctic and use kayaks, not open canoes, learned this long ago.) This may either prevent a swamping in the first instance or else if you do turn over and have to bail out, hold your gear together and keep the canoe more buoyant for a while. Secondly, have a very long rope, 100 feet or more on a least one end of every canoe. The rope itself should float or have a float tied at the end and a "handle" for an easy grab. With such a rope one can swim to shore with the handle and effect a self-rescue. Or failing that, the rescue canoe can take the long rope, paddle to shore quickly with it and then from shore haul-in by hand the swamped canoe, with the people hanging on it. Towing a swamped canoe to shore by paddling another canoe is very slow and exhausting and should only be done if no other alternative exists. Thirdly, always carry a gas stove and an emergency supply of fuel in reserve for such an accident above the tree line.   It allows one to quickly generate heat and warmth, albeit in limited form. Fourthly, carry an emergency EPIRB, sewn into a pocket on your lifejacket, so that, should you swamp and lose everything else, if you make it to shore (and are wearing the lifejacket) you could turn it on and then try to stay alive until the rescue takes place. These are the four most basic survival lessons I learned from Art's article and from my first trip into the Barrens.

On weekend trips in the south I have dumped countless times while learning whitewater skills and attempting rapids beyond by ability. But in all my years of northern canoeing I have only swamped twice on wilderness trips, both in much warmer conditions than in the Moffatt case, and with no real penalty. Both were the result of carelessness, a case of not paying enough attention to approaching rocks. Both times a self rescue was quite easy. Once we were pinned on a rock in shallow water in NW Ontario and I could walk to shore. The other time, in 1972, it was at a run-out of a rapid on the Riviere de Pas in Quebec. In this case, while swimming in deep water, I simply grabbed the loop at the end of my long stern rope and swam to shore with it. As soon as I touched bottom I pulled on the rope, and the canoe, at the other end of the rope, swung into shore. The snap-on spray cover kept all the packs inside the canoe and, except for minor wetting and the embarrassment of it all, no harm was done.

I like to say that I don't need luck to come back safely from canoeing in the north. Instead, what I do need is the absence of bad luck. There is a major difference. Needing luck to me implies incompetence or the taking of unnecessary risk. But with all the competence and judgment in the world, some risk cannot be avoided. In particular one can always imagine an unlucky combination of wind and water and cold that traps one in a hopeless situation. The possibility of being a casualty of bad luck is the unavoidable price of living.

To offset the fear of bad luck, in an encounter with a marauding bear or the loss of food in a dump, some advocate bringing guns on canoe trips into the Barrens. I don't. Art Moffatt did not bring a gun with him and I admire him immensely for this. His younger bowmen did bring guns.

Today, in 1995, I cannot imagine canoeists bringing guns on trips to try and live off the land by shooting caribou, as the Moffatt party did forty years ago. That was a different time and era. It should not be repeated today. A fishing rod and lures is as far as I would go to supplement the food you bring with you. After their dump, the Moffatt party lost both guns, and their only recourse to starvation was a speedy exit. In a serious emergency if you lose all your food supply, an EPIRB and an ensuing rescue are a better alternative.

What about firearms for protection? This is more controversial. My own choice is not to bring a gun on Barren Land trips. In my view I am more at risk from shooting myself accidentally and the bears are more at risk from my shooting them unnecessarily, than there is any real danger from bears. To have something, I do bring pepper spray, or "Bear-Guard", with me. In the eight trips and 200 days in the Barrens to date, I have only seen the barren land grizzly some five or six times, and in every case it ran off. Our imagination often confuses "possibility" with "probability". Almost anything imaginable is possible. The real issue is whether it is probable enough to warrant concern.

I have taken a gun on two canoe trips, both times when I canoed in northernmost Labrador, where polar bears can abound in summer. My gun was a 12 gauge shotgun with a 5-shot magazine and the first two or three shots being plastic balls, which is a deterrent, and only the remaining shots are lethal lead slugs. The plastic balls do not penetrate, only thump the bear. Fortunately I have never had to use the gun to test out their effectiveness. A kayaking friend however had the experience in Labrador of a polar bear aggressively attacking a tent in the middle of the night with a person sleeping inside. In self-defence they shot the polar bear.

The gun issue concerns me. If many of the ever increasing numbers of wilderness canoeists carry guns, the bears will be endangered. We are the endangering species, not the bears. The larger mammals are inexorably being pushed off the surface of the planet by man in competition for space. In the larger scheme of things it is of no consequence if a few of us canoeists are casualties to rogue bears. The greater loss arises if we are party to their demise as a species. Perhaps we canoeists should not go into a wilderness area if we are not willing to assume the minimal risk of encountering the rare rogue bear that sees us as part of its food chain.

I cannot help but sense that somewhere, ages ago, with the invention of steel and gunpowder, we broke a sacred covenant with the natural world around us. Up till then there had been a balance between man and the other carnivores. Each could kill the other. It ceased being so when man acquired a gun and at long range, turned it on his fellow creatures. Ever since then we have butchered species after species with our technological advantage. When the Europeans arrived in North America, the Native people were likewise seduced by the immediate advantages of hunting with guns. They too broke the covenant with the animal world.

Art Moffatt was remarkable in this regard. George Grinnell's description of his encounter with the barren ground grizzly will become a mythical legend and cause a lot of campers around an evening fire to shake their heads in disbelief as they talk about it. With a bear charging him, Art's first thought was for the bear's safety. He was afraid, not for himself, but that one of his "gunmen" would shoot it. He was already practising a wilderness ethic that placed the bear's importance above his own. I don't believe I could do that, though I wish I could.

Appreciation

Art's journey ended in death, and so did, unfortunately, the journey of my sons; all journeys end in death; it is the nature of the human pilgrimage; but there is another point: part of Art's journey and the journey of my sons lives on. It lives on in me, and it lives on in others. For a long time I thought I was the only one carrying it on, but one day I received a call from George Luste inviting me to tell the story of Art's expedition at the annual Wilderness Canoe Symposium.

On the last weekend in January, eleven years ago, George Luste had invited some canoeing friends into his living room for a "slidefest" in order to reminisce about past trips. His living room overflowed, and so next year he rented an auditorium, which also overflowed, and the next year a larger auditorium, and the year after that a larger one still. Each year for the last ten years, canoeists from all over the world have been making another kind of pilgrimage. This one to Toronto in the middle of winter.

I thought I had been alone all these years as Art had been alone in his desire to share the beauty and truth of the wilderness with others; but in that packed auditorium, I realized how wrong I was. I could feel Art's spirit live on amongst these canoeists. George Luste invited me back for the ten year retrospective last year. I told the story again in longer form, and he urged me to write this book; others at that Symposium did also: Bob Henderson, Allan Brown, Robert Perkins, Seth Feldman, Mavis Brown.... I am grateful for all their support.

Forty years ago, I told the story of Art's trip to a friend, Edward Chalfant, who was a Professor of English literature at work on a biography of Henry Adams. He told me to put the story in print, and then he handed me his typewriter.

The first time I wrote the book, it was rejected by Viking Press. The second time, it was rejected by Harper's, the third time, it was rejected by Duell, Sloan and Pearce, the fourth time by Doublday Canada, the fifth time by the House of Anansi, the sixth time by Norton.... Every time the manuscript was rejected, I rewrote it, and I hope made it better; but I never seemed to get it right, and after forty years I was beginning to get discouraged.

George Luste recommended an agent, Diane Bukowski. She said the story was worth telling, but recommended I enlist the help of a professional writer. I had tried that. My aunt published poetry under the name, Lisa Grenelle; she had been named "poet of the year" by the *New York Herald Tribune* and taught writing at the Carnegie Institute, but even with her help, I could not find a publisher.

Finally George Luste said that if all else failed, he would publish it and would distribute it to his canoeing friends through Northern Books, a sideline enterprise of his. With his encouragement I tried one more time to tell the story, and this time I believe I have told it as it ought to have been told before. Maybe I needed forty years to reflect on the meaning of the experience; maybe the manuscript needed to be rejected by seven publishers; or maybe this time the right combination of people came together; but whatever, I believe I have at last written a good book.

George Luste and I corresponded a good deal while I was writing it. He helped me see the adventure from different perspectives, and many chapters were rewritten because of his comments. At the end of our correspondence, I think we have come to similar, if not identical, conclusions.

Today, I still have a longing to go back to that beautiful wilderness, and when I meditate on death, my soul still seeks its spiritual home there. At the same time, I agree with George that it is possible to achieve a spiritual relationship with the wilderness without dying young. Spray covers help.

Down east in Cape Breton, Laurie introduced me to Wilf Cude. He had been an officer in the Canadian Navy who decided to get a PhD in English literature, but he ran foul of his PhD committee. He published his dissertation to favorable reviews. The Dean recommended that the dissertation be defended, but Wilf's PhD committee dug in its heels, and so with an AbD. (all but dissertation), Wilf floated around the fringes of Academia. One Spring, he sat down and wrote the *PhD Trap*. It was rejected by James Lorrimer, who told Wilf that it would never sell. Wilf pulled out his Visa card and printed 500 copies, which were sold within six weeks. He printed up a thousand more, and they were soon snapped up, then another thousand, and so Wilf decided to go into publishing under the name of Medicine Label Press.

When he read an early draft of *A Death on the Barrens*, he became interested in joining the venture and took on the job of editor. The book is a great deal easier to read today than it was when I first handed it to him. The restructuring of a sentence, the removal of a redundant phrase, the choice of a more meaningful word, take patience and skill. Wilf is an excellent editor who knows how to draw the best out of a writer, and I have enjoyed working with him.

I contacted Creigh Moffatt, Art's daughter, to ask for permission to quote from Art's diary, of which she holds the copyright. Creigh, with her husband, a champion kayaker, and her son, who is following in the family tradition, now lives up the same dirt road in the same house that her parents, Carol and Art Moffatt, once lived. The summer Art died, Creigh had just turned four, but she remembers him fondly and has inherited his love of the outdoors. She was able to fill in some of the details about Art's war experience with the American Field Service, and, as a professional editor herself, made a number of helpful suggestions. I have really enjoyed talking with her about Art on the phone. We share a mutual admiration for the man.

I believe that the book has been deepened through my correspondence with George Luste, has been made more readable by Wilf Cude's editing, has been made more true to Art's spirit through my correspondence and conversations with Creigh Moffatt; but it is to Laurie that I owe the most. She has endured the eccentricities which the trip left me with (40 degree temperatures in the home, a love of boiled mouldy food, a detachment from civilization). She has encouraged and supported the project all the way through; she has insisted that I meet with those who could help bring the book to fruition; she has acted as a buffer zone between me and people at large; she has helped the marriage survive four a.m. panic attacks, my fragile temperment, endless readings and rewritings of the manuscript, and she has laid aside her own work for four years so the book could be published. I am most grateful to her for an eleventh hour rescue operation on Chapter Twelve on the Caribou. In Chapter Twelve, I had launched a mini-PhD dissertation on the sins of the American Empire, which Wilf had, at first, objected to, then had gamely played along with; but Laurie dug her heels into the chapter and brought it back into focus once again with the reminder that it was I, not America, who was unable to both "march and dance at the same time (her phrase)." Generally speaking, she kept her hands off the details, but kept the essence of me and the book on track.

And so with the support of George Luste, Wilf Cude, Creigh Moffatt and Laurie, the book has come together.

Other Acknowledgements

Quotes from Arthur Moffatt's Journal are taken from the *Sports Illustrated* article that appeared in the March 9th and March 16th, 1959 issues. Art's Journal was abridged by the editors of *Sports Illustrated*. The original, unabridged, journal resides in the Dartmouth Library. The copyright is held by Creigh Moffatt and is quoted with her permission. Joe Lanouette's account of the accident can be found in the *Sports Illustrated* article.

The expression, "paved over paradise with a parking lot," was common around Berkeley, California when I was taking my PhD between 1962-1967. Creigh Moffatt reminded me that its origin probably lies with Joni Mitchell: "...paved paradise and put up a parking lot."

The quote, "...miles and miles of nothing but miles and miles," is a common description of the Barrens, but I have lost the original reference.

Photographs of the Barrens were taken mainly by George Luste and other members of his expedition in 1969, particularly Richard Irwin and Robert Herendeen. Photographs of our trip in 1955 were published previously in the *Sports Illustrated* article of March 9th, and 16th, 1955.

"Those who go to the Arctic once, write a book; those who go twice, stay." - Author unknown

Select Bibliography On the Barrens, the Arctic and Canoeing (From Northern Books)

Professor Luste

Part I. In-print titles (1995)

BACK, George [Edited by C. Stuart Houston. Commentary by I.S. MacLaren]; *Arctic Artist*: The Journal and Paintings of George Back, Midshipman with Franklin, 1819-1822. McGill-Queens, 1995, 392p, 40 colour, 10 b&w photos. First publication of journal. Cloth.

BERTON, Pierre; *Mysterious North*. McClelland & Stewart, 391p. Sections on Nahanni, Klondike, Labrador, Barrens. Cloth.

BERTON, Pierre; *The Arctic Grail*: The Quest for the North West Passage and the North Pole, 1818-1909. McClelland & Stewart, 672p, many maps; bibliography, index. Highly recommended as an excellent initial overview of the subject. Cloth.

BROWNING, Peter; *The Last Wilderness*. Great West, 1989, 192p, photos. 600 mile canoe trip from Black Lake to Snowdrift. Pb.

BURT, Page; *Barrenland Beauties*: Showy Plants of the Arctic Coast. Outcrop, 246p, 200 colour photos. Practical guide. Pb.

CONOVER, Garrett; *Beyond the Paddle*: A Canoeist's Guide to Expedition Skills; Poling, Lining, Portaging, and Maneuvering through Ice. Old Bridge Press, 105p. Pb.

CONOVER, Garrett & Alexandra; *A Snow Walker's Companion*: Winter Trail Skills from the Far North. Ragged Mountain Press, 238p. Pb.

FRANKLIN, Sir John; *Thirty Years in the Arctic Regions*. U of Nebraska. Reprint of 1859 original. 480p. Pb.

HALL, Ed. [Editor]; *People and the Caribou*: In the Northwest Territories. Twenty-one contributors, with material organized in four sections; People, Science, Barren Ground Caribou, and Other Caribou. Pb.

HALSEY, David, [with Diana Landau]; *Magnetic North*: A Trek across Canada from the Pacific to the Atlantic by Foot, Dogsled and Canoe. 252p. Cloth & pb.

HAMILTON, John David; *Arctic Revolution*: Social Change in the Northwest Territories, 1935-1994. Dundurn, 298p. Pb.

HODGINS, Bruce W. & Gwyneth Hoyle; *Canoeing North into the Unknown*: A Record of River Travel; 1874-1974. Natural Heritage, 279p, photos, maps. Account of many river systems, history, geography, and a chronological record of canoeists. Pb.

HODGINS, Bruce W. & M. Hobbs [Editors]; *Nastawgan*. Betelgeuse, 231p. Essays on canoe, snowshoe, wilderness, etc. Pb.

HOOD, Robert [Edited by C. Stuart Houston]; *To the Arctic by Canoe*: The Journal and Paintings of Robert Hood, Midshipman with Franklin. McGill-Queens, 280p, 24 colour illustrations, 5 maps. Weakened by starvation, Hood was shot through the head by a member of the party. Pb.

INGSTAD, Heige; *The Land of Feast and Famine*. McGill-Queens. Reprint of 1933 northern classic on the Barrens, northeast of Great Slave Lake. Pb.

JACOBSON, Cliff; *Canoeing Wild Rivers*. ICS, 355p, illustr. Complete how-to-book. Misrepresents the Moffatt tragedy. Pb.

JAMES, William C; *A Fur Trader's Photographs*: A.A. Chesterfield in the District of Ungava 1901-1904. McGill-Queens. Cloth.

JASON, Victoria; *Kabloona in a Yellow Kayak*: One Woman's Journey Through the Northwest Passage. Cloth.

KESSELHEIM, Alan S; *Water and Sky*: Reflections of a Northern Year. Stoddart, 311p. Canoe travel from Jasper to Baker Lake via Lake Athabaska, to the Dubawnt River and via the Kazan River to Baker Lake. Cloth.

KLEIN, Clayton; *Cold Summer Wind*. Wilderness Adventure, 277p. Narrative of a father and son canoeing team who have traveled many NWT rivers, including the Kazan, Elk-Thelon, and Back River. Cloth.

LEDEN, Christian [Tr. by L. Neatby]; *Across the Keewatin Ice-Field*: Three Years Among the Canadian Eskimo 1913-1916. Watson and Dwyer, 298p, illustr. Pb.

MARTYN, Katharine; J.B. Tyrrell: *Explorer and Adventurer*: The Geological Survey Years, 1881-1898. Thomas Fisher Library, 72p, illustr. Pb.

MASON, Bill; *Path of the Paddle*. Key Porter, 208p. Illustrated guide to the Art of Canoeing. Lg pb.

MASON, Bill; *Song of the Paddle*. Key Porter, 186p. Illustrated guide to Wilderness Camping. Lg pb.

McCREADIE, Mary [Ed]; *Canoeing Canada's Northwest Territories*. CRCA, 1995, 194p. Pb.

MERRICK, Elliott; *True North*. U of Nebraska, 353p, illustr. Living and travelling in Labrador. Reprint of 1933 original. Northern classic. Pb.

MORSE, Eric W; *Freshwater Saga*: Memoirs of a Lifetime of Wilderness Canoeing in Canada. U of Toronto, 189p, illustr. Pb.

NOEL, Lynn E. [Editor]; *Voyages*: Canada's Heritage Rivers. Maps and illustrations by Hap Wilson. Breakwater. Includes the Kazan, Thelon, Seal, etc. Cloth.

NORMENT, Christopher; *In the North of Our Lives*: A year in the wilderness of Northern Canada. Down East, 248p, illustr. From the Macmillan in the Yukon to the shores of Hudson Bay, near Chesterfield, in August 1978. Fine read. Cloth.

OLESEN, David; *North of Reliance*: *Wilderness living on Great Slave Lake*. Northwood, 160p, ilustr. Pb.

PELLY, David F. & C.C. Hanks [Editors]; *The Kazan: Journey Into an Emerging Land*. 135p, illustr. Part river journal, part natural history. Pb.

PIELO, E.C.; *A Naturalist's Guide to the Arctic*. U of Chicago, 327p, illustr. Recommended. Pb.

RAFFAN, James & B. Horwood [Editors]; *Canexus*: The Canoe in Canadian culture. Betelgeuse, 212p. Essays from conference. Pb.

RAFFAN, James; *Summer North of Sixty*: By Paddle and Portage across the Barren Lands. Key Porter, 229p. Burnside River. Cloth.

RICHARDSON, John [Edited by C. Stuart Houston]; *The Journal of John Richardson*, Surgeon-Naturalist with Franklin 1820-1822. Illustrated by H. Albert Hachbaum. McGill-Queens, 349p. First publication of Richardson's journal. Lg cloth and pb editions.

STARKELL, Don; *Paddle to the Arctic*. McClelland & Stewart. Cloth.

WALKER, Marilyn; *Harvesting the Northern Wild*: A guide to Traditional and Contemporary uses of Edible Forest Plants in the Northwest Territories. Outcrop, 224p, illustr. Pb.

WIEBE, RUDY; *A Discovery of Strangers*. Knopf Canada, 317p. maps. Historical fiction about the First Franklin Expedition. It won the Governor General's Award in 1994. Cloth.

WIEBE, Rudy; *Playing Dead*: A Contemplation Concerning the Arctic. New West, 123p. Pb.

WILSON, Ian & Sally; *Arctic Adventures*: Exploring Canada's North by Canoe and Dog Team. Gordon Soules, 246p, illustr. One year and 3500 kilometers of travel across Canada's vast Arctic by a young couple. Pb.

Part II. Out-of-print titles (1995) - may be located via used and antiquarian booksellers.

BACK, Capt. George; *Narrative of the Arctic Land Expedition*: To the Mouth of the Great Fish River and along the Shores of the Arctic Ocean in the Years 1833, 1834, and 1835. 1836, London and later, 1979 Hurtig reprint, 663 pages, illustrations, maps. Back's expedition in 1833-34-35 to the Arctic Ocean via what today is the Back River, complete with large folding map.

BARKER, Bertram; *North of '53*: the Adventures of a Trapper and Prospector in the Canadian Far North. London. 1934c, 242p. Covers the area north of Flin Flon as far as Chesterfield Inlet.

BIRKET-SMITH, Kaj; *The Eskimos*. London, Methuen, 1959, 262p, endpaper map, many illustrations, appendicies, extensive bibliography. This is a revised and extended edition of the 1936 classic work. Covers all Eskimo tribes from Greenland to the Bering Straits, including the Caribou Eskimo of the Kazan. Birket-Smith spent a number of years in the north and was an important member of Rasmusson's Thule expeditions. A valuable source of information.

BLANCHET, Guy; *Search in the North*. Toronto, Macmillan, 197p, photos, map. Blanchet was a well traveled northern authority on the Great Slave Lake area and the Barrens, canoeing and exploring in the days of John Hornby. He narrates the story of the first use of an aeroplane in the search for minerals and the search for the MacAlpine party in the barrens (1928 and 1929).

BOAS, Franz; *The Central Eskimo*. Coles reprint of 1888 original. Toronto, 1974, 401-675pp. "The following account of the Central Eskimo contains chiefly the results of the author's own observations and collections made during his 1883-84 sojourn on Baffin Island and to Cumberland Strait and Davis Inlet, supplemented by extracts from the reports of other travellers."

BREYNAT, Mgr. Gabriel, O.M.J.; *The Flying Bishop*: Fifty years in the Canadian Far North. London 1955, xii, 288p 8vo, endpaper maps, illustrations. The author was in a position to give authentic facts concerning the tragic fate of Fr. Rouviere and Fr. Le Roux.

BRUEMMER, Fred; *The Arctic*. This and numerous other titles by a highly respected photographer and writer on the arctic.

CALEB, George; *Caribou and the Barren Lands*. Toronto, Firefly, 1981c, 176 p, bibliography. A well-written, superbly illustrated book on the caribou of the far north. A fine book.

CHRISTIAN, Edgar; *Unflinching - A Diary of Tragic Adventure*. John Murray, 1937, 156 p. The tragic and gripping diary of nineteen year old Christian, cousin of John Hornby, who was the third and last to die of starvation on the Thelon River in June of 1927. He wrote till he no longer had the strength to hold a pencil and knew the end was near.

CLARKE, C.H.D; *A Biological Investigation of the Thelon Game Sanctuary*. *Ottawa*, 1940, 135p, 3 folding maps, illustrations, bibliography with 200 entries. Author, with W.H.B. Hoare, visited the Thelon Game Sanctuary in 1937 for the National Museum and this is the report. An excellent reference booklet for the Thelon River, its history and wildlife.

DOUGLAS, George M; *Lands Forlorn*: A Story of an Expedition to Hearne's Coppermine River. New York, G.P. Putnam's, 1914, 285p, many plates (about 180), 2 folding maps at end. Douglas and his two companions journeyed to the Dease River on Great Bear Lake, wintered there and made two trips to the Coppermine River, one to the Arctic coast. A profusely illustrated book. Douglas first met Hornby when he was living and travelling on Great Bear.

DOWNES, P.G; *Sleeping Island*. Originally published in 1943, reprinted in 1988. Classic narrative of 1939 canoe trip north of Reindeer Lake to Nueltin and the edge of the barrens.

FRANKLIN, John; *Narrative of a Journey to the Shores of the Polar Sea, in the years 1819, 20, 21, and 22*: With an Appendix on Various Subjects Relating to Science and Natural History. 1823 and later reprint editions, such as 1970 Hurtig. The account of one of the most famous and difficult early expeditions to the Canadian arctic. Franklin was accompanied by John Richardson, George Back, and Robert Hood. Their expedition reached the Arctic Ocean on July 18, 1821 via the Coppermine River, verifying Hearne's Bloody Falls. They then travelled eastward in two canoes, surveying about 340 km of intricate ice-infested shoreline. On their return trip they ascended Hood River and after much hardship reached their winter quarters at Fort Enterprise. Hood was murdered during the return trek and about 10 of the boatmen died of starvation.

FRANKLIN, John; *Narrative of a Second Expedition to the Shores of the Polar Sea in the Years 1825, 1826, and 1827*. 1828 and later reprints, such as 1971 edition, 320p, clvii, 31 full page plates, 6 folding maps in rear pocket.

GAPEN, Dan D. Sr.; *Fishing Rivers of the Far North*, with illustrations by Margaret Caldwell. Privately printed, [nd], 337p, colour plates - on the Kazan, Ogoki, Thelon, Albany, Talston. Primarily a fishing book, written by an outdoor and fishing professional. Discusses many of the great northern rivers.

GILDER, William H.; *Schwatka's Search*: Sledging in the Arctic in Quest of the Franklin Records. 1881, 316p, two colour maps, illustrations, index, glossary. In 1879-80, Schwatka and his party explored the overland route from Daley Bay (near Wager Inlet on Hudson Bay) to King William Island, north of the Back River. A fine read.

HANBURY, David T; *Sport and Travel in the Northland of Canada*. N.Y. Macmillan, 1904, 319p, col. fron, illustr, 36 plates (4 col), 2 foldout maps. Narrative of the experiences of the author and two companions, living and travelling with the native Inuit in the Barren Lands of Canada, 1901-02, for some 20 months. Hanbury's travels extended from Hudson Bay to the Mackenzie River and from Great Slave Lake to the Arctic coast. An exceptional northern travel narrative. (That somehow was never reprinted!)

HARPELLE, Alix; *Those Were the Days That I Lived and Loved*: biography of Gus D'Aoust, a professional barrenland trapper. Privately printed. 1988, 215p. Gus D'Aoust, born in 1896, spent most of his long life trapping east of Great Slave Lake, near Fort Reliance and into the Barrens.

HARPER, Francis; *Caribou Eskimo of the Upper Kazan River in Keewatin*. U of Kansas, 1964, 72 p, photo plates, notes, bibliography. Harper spent six month, in 1947, living at a trading post on Nueltin Lake. Harper describes Charles Schweder's efforts to assist the starving Caribou Eskimo.

HARRINGTON, Richard; *The Face of the Arctic*: A Cameraman's Story in Words and Pictures of the Far North. NY; Schuman, 1952, lg 8vo, 369 p, profusely illustrated with author's photos. From 1947 to 1951, the author/photographer travelled the remote corners of the Canadian arctic recording his observations in words and pictures. His powerful photos of the starving Padleimiuts, near Padlei in the barrens, also appeared in acclaimed photographic collection; 'The Family of Man'.

HAYDON, A.L.; *The Riders of the Plains*: A Record of the Royal North-West Mounted Police of Canada 1873-1910. 1973 Hurtig reprint of 1910 original. 385p. Includes a brief description of Inspector R. F. Pelletier's 3,347 mile patrol in 1908 from Fort Saskatchewan to Great Slave Lake, across the Barrens via the Thelon River and down the coast of Hudson Bay to Fort Churchill.

HEARNE, Samuel; *A Journey from Prince of Wales's Fort in Hudson's Bay, to the Northern Ocean:* Undertaken by Order of the Hudson's Bay Company for the Discovery of Copper Mines, a North-West Passage. &c. in the Years 1769, 1770, 1771, & 1772. 1795 and later reprint editions, such as 1971 Hurtig. Hearne was the Marco Polo of Northern Canada and the first white man to reach the Arctic Ocean by land. His first two starts were unsuccessful. He then joined with Matonabbee, a Chipewayan, and his encampment, to travel to Bloody Falls at the mouth of the Coppermine River. Hearne left Prince of Wales Fort (now Churchill) on December 7, 1770 and returned June 30, 1772, after an absence of some 19 months. His journey demonstrated that there was no hope of a low latitude North-west Passage. In his travels he 'discovered' Great Slave Lake, and gathered much information on natural history and the indigenous natives.

HEARNE, Samuel [edited by Richard Glover]; *A Journey to the Northern Ocean.* 1958, 301p, illustrations, folding map, index. A popular edition of this northern classic. Historian Glover provides an informative 43 page introduction.

HOARE, W.H.B.; *Journal of a Barrenlander (1928-1929).* Edited and annotated by Sheila C. Thomson. 1990, 186p, maps, index. In Jaunary 1928 Billy Hoare was assigned by Ottawa to investigate the Thelon Game Sanctuary in the NWT. He and Knox carried out this very demanding assignment and wintered at "Warden's Grove" on the Thelon River, a few miles upstream fo the Hornby cabin. This is a record of his daily journal, written at the time.

HUDSON'S BAY CO.; *Beaver Magazine.* Started in the 1920's by the Hudson's Bay Company, this fine magazine has untold excellent northern articles and stories. It no longer is owned by the HBC.

INGLIS, Alex; *Northern Vagabond*: The Life and Career of J.B. Tyrrell. Toronto, 1978, 8vo, 256p, maps and illustrations. The first full career biography of Joseph Burr Tyrrell, the man who traversed the barrens twice, in 1893 via the Dubawnt River and again in 1894 via the Kazan River.

IRWIN, David; *One Man Against the North*: Alone with dogs, in 1935 the 24-year-old author travelled 3600 miles across the top of the world, including the Barren Lands.

KEMP, H.S.M.; *Northern Trader.* London, 1957, 8vo, 239p. In 1908, at the age of sixteen, the author went to Lac La Ronge to work as clerk for the Hudson Bay Company and stayed in the North until 1928. He travelled and worked throughout the North, learned Cree, and writes a good narrative.

LAMB, W. Kaye [Ed.]; *The Journals and Letters of Sir Alexander Mackenzie.* Cambridge Univ Press, 1970, 551p, several folding maps and illustrations. Dr. Lamb provides a lengthy introduction and notes on both of Mackenzie's journals and letters written between 1786 and 1819. The letters provide additional information about his character and career in the fur trade. The comprehensive volume on Mackenzie.

MALLET, Captain Thierry; *Plain Tales of the North*. 1925, 136 pages, illustrated with sketches. For twenty-five years the author inspected the northern trading posts of Revillon Freres. This is his first and scarcer, of two books. It includes fifty tales of the north, from 'A Grave in Saskatchewan' to 'The Call of the Wild North of Fifty-Three'.

MALLET, Captain Thierry; *Glimpses of the Barren Lands*. 1930, 142p. Seven stories and a barren land favourite. Mallet, head of Revillon Freres, was a sympathetic observer of the north and the barrens. The title comes from one of the seven chapters. The last one is title 'When Caribou Failed'.

MALLORY, Enid; *Coppermine*: The Far North of George M. Douglas. 273p, illustr. Lg cloth.

MARSH, Donald B.; *Canada's Caribou Eskimos*. 18 page article in the complete issue of National Geographic, January 1947. The Padlermiut [people of the willow thicket] west of Arviat [Eskimo Point] as their ancient customs disappear.

MARSH, Winifred P.; *People of the Willow*: The Padlimiut Tribe of the Caribou Eskimo. 1976, 63p. Twenty-five watercolour paintings of the native way of life near Eskimo Point and the Barrens in 1933. Colourful, sensitive and fascinating.

McCOURT, Edward; *The Yukon and the Northwest Territories*. 1969, 236p, 24 photos, index. The

Canadian north in history and legend. An excellent chapter on the Barren Lands, with some inspiring, eloquent writing; "Why do men go to the Barren Lands?..."

MORICE, Rev. Adrian G.; *Thawing Out the Eskimo*. Translated by Mary T. Loughlin. Boston Society for the Propagation of the Faith, 1943c, 241p, photos. The biography of bishop Turquetil, who lived in the land of ice and snow for thirty years - among the Eskimos of Hudson Bay to northern Baffin Island, with narratives on the founding and development of missions at Chesterfield Inlet, Southampton Island, Baker Lake, Pond Inlet and Igloolik.

MOWAT, Farley; *Canada North*. 1967, 128p. An excellent general overview of the Canadian North in words and pictures - for example, it has a fine summary of the main arctic flowers in coloured photos.

MOWAT, Farley; *The People of the Deer*. 952, 320 p. Semi-fiction, the sympathetic and eloquent portrayal of the Caribou Eskimo of the Kazan River barrens, based on a 1947 visit.

MOWAT, Farley; *The Desperate People*. 1959 and later reprints, 305p. The sequel to the "People of the Deer" and a more carefully documented book.

MOWAT, Farley; Tundra: *Selections from the Great Accounts of Arctic Land Voyages*. Toronto, 1973, 416p, photos, maps, illus. This volume deals with the European penetration into the Arctic land mass. Includes chapters on Hearne, Mackenzie, Franklin, Back, Tyrrell, Stefansson, Hornby, Mallet, etc. An excellent introduction to the sub-arctic. Vol III of trilogy.

MOWAT, Farley; *The Snow Walker*. 1978, 222p. Author "presents a memorable portrait of a land and its people, capturing the essence of the Arctic and of Eskimo lore." (dj quote).

MOYLES, R.G.; *British Law and Arctic Men*: The Celebrated 1917 Murder Trails of Sinnisiak and Uluksuk, First Inuit Trial under White Man's Rule. 1979, 93p, photos, notes, short bibliography. The classic arctic story of cultural clash between the native and white people. First in the form of two white priests who are killed in the barren landscape near the Coppermine River and later again in the white man's court of law. Story includes John Hornby and George Douglas who knew the missionaries at Great Bear Lake.

NANSEN, Fridtjof; *Farthest North*: Being the Record of a Voyage of Exploration of the Ship "Fram" 1893-1896 and of the Fifteen Months' Sleigh Journey by Dr Nansen and Lt. Johansen. With an Appendix by Otto Sverdrup, Captain of the Fram. NY & Lon, Harper, 1897 vol 1 at 587 p, vol 2 at 729 p, teg, many illustrations, 16 colour plates, 4 maps in pocket, index.

OLSON, Sigurd F.; *The Lonely Land*, illustrated by Francis Lee Jaques. NY, 1961, 273 pages. Description of a five hundred miles canoe trip along the Churchill River in northern Saskastchewan retracing the voyageur route to Cumberland House. A very enjoyable read.

OSGOOD, Cornelius; *Winter*, With decorations by Jean Day. NY, W.W.Norton, 1953, London, 8vo, 255p, endpaper map. Mint copy in dj. Great Bear Lake and Great Bear River area. "The intimate experience of a lone man in the far north - a strange and haunting story unique in the literature of personal adventure."

PEARCE, Richard; *Marooned in the Arctic*: The Diary of the MacAlpine Dominion Explorers Expedition of 1929. [Toronto, privately printed, 1931], 71p, 6 plates, incl map. "Printed by the author in the office of the Northern Miner, in a small edition, one copy for each of the eight members of the expedition and a few additional copies. Contains the day-by-day account of the flight from Churchill to Baker Lake, the forced landing at Dease Point in the Bathurst Inlet region..."

PERCHER, Kamil; *Lonely Voyage*: By Kayak to Adventure and Discovery. 1978, 185 pages, photos. An introspective 600 mile solo journey along the fur trade rivers of northern Saskatchewan.

PELLY, David F.; *Expedition*: An Arctic Journey through History on George Back's River. Toronto, Betelgeuse, 1981, xiii, 172p, maps, illustrations. A

1977 canoe expedition the length of the Back River. Several interesting historical sketches by Capt. George Back.

PERKINS, Robert; *Into the Great Solitude*. An Arctic Journey. An eloquent narrative of two journeys - the 750 solo miles down the Back River; and the solitary inner journey of a poet. A very good read.

PIKE, Warburton; *Barren Ground of Northern Canada. 1892*, 300p. Classic narrative of early travel and hunting in the region north of the east end of Great Slave Lake, in 1889-91. Includes descriptions of the country and the life of the Indians among whom he camped. Concludes with the eloquent answer by Saltatha to the priest on the beauty of the Barren Ground.

PREBLE, Edward A.; *A Biological Investigation of Hudson Bay Region. U.S. Department of Agriculture*, North American Fauna, report #22. Washington, 1902, 8vo, 140p, wraps, map, 14 photo plates, extensive bibliography. Preble travelled by canoe from Norway House to Fort Churchill and to Eskimo Point in 1900. And then back. He lists "Mammals of Keewatin" and "Birds of Keewatin".

RAFFAN, James [Ed.]; *Wild Waters*: Canoeing Canada's Wilderness Rivers. Key Porter, 1986, 152 pages, many superb colour photos. A coffee-table book about nine wilderness rivers.

RASMUSSEN, Knud;   *Across Arctic America: Narrative of the Fifth Thule Expedition.* New York & London, Putnam's 1927, 388p, with 64 illustrations and 4 maps.   Starting from Greenland, Knud Rasmussen sledged backward over the epic migration route of ancient man from Siberia.   An amazing narrative. Eloquant and informative.

RUSSELL, Frank; *Explorations in the Far North*: Being the Report of an expedtion Under the Auspices of the University of Iowa during the years 1892, 93, and 94., 1898, 290p, folding map, 21 plates, index. Narrative of the author's journey to his base at Fort Rae, his life with the Indians, winter travel, musk oxen, in the Great Slave Lake region and north, as well as eastward into the Barren Ground. Detailed observations on a variety of topics.

SETON, Ernest Thompson; *The Arctic Prairies*: A Canoe Journey of 2,000 miles in Search of the Caribou, being the account of a voyage to the region north of Aylmer lake [in NWT].   1912 and later reprints, 415p, numerous photos, illustrations. The account of author's trip with A.E. Preble in 1907. Includes thorough notes and descriptions of the wildlife, characteristics of the landscape and life on the trail, east of Great Slave Lake.

SPEARS, Borden [Editor]; *Wilderness Canada. Photographs assembled by Bruce M. Litteljohn. 1970,* 174 pages. Eight contributions, including Pierre Elliot Trudeau's "Exhaustion and Fulfilment. The

Ascetic in a Canoe" and Eric Morse's "Challenge and Response, the Modern Voyageur".

STEELE, Harwood; *Policing the Arctic*: the Story of the Conquest of the Arctic by the Royal Canadian (formerly North-West) Mounted Police. 1936, 390p, 31 plates, large folding map, index. Account, based on official records and personal knowledge, of Dominion police work in the Yukon from the time of the Klondike gold rush, police patrols, rescue work, manhunts, etc. in various regions of the Canadian North. Includes the Force's long patrol across the barrens in 1977, after the Radford and Street murders. From Baker Lake to Bernard Habour and back (5153 miles). A bibliography/source material is listed for each of the 41 chapters. Much RCMP information. The fold out map indicates most northerly posts and detachments in 1894, 1902 and 1926.

STONEHOUSE, Bernard; *Animals of the Arctic*: The Ecology of the Far North. New York. New York, 1971, 172 pages, many excellent colour photos. The author, a biologist, has worked in the arctic. Great photographs.

TYRRELL, J. Burr; *Report of the Doobaunt*, Kazan, and Ferguson Rivers: And the North-West coast of Hudson Bay and on Two Overland Routes from Hudson Bay to Lake Winnipeg. Geological Survey of Canada Annual Report, 1897, 218p, plates, folding map. A classic barren land survey. Several photos by J.B. and a large fold-out map showing his 1893 & 1894 routes, with portages indicated.

TYRRELL, J. W.; *Across the Sub-Arctics of Canada*: A Journey of 3,200 miles by canoe and snowshoe through the Barren Lands. 1898, and later Coles reprint, 280p, illustrated and folding map, drawings by Arthur Heming and J.S. Gordon. The northern classic describes the trip led by J.B. Tyrrell across the barrens, via the Dubawnt River to Baker Lake. Includes their near tragedy in racing winter down the coast of Hudson Bay.

WALDRON, Malcolm; *Snow Man*: John Hornby in the Barren Lands; 1931, 292p. frontis, illustr, endpaper map. Based on the diaries and records of J.C. Crtichell-Bullock, the story of the journey made by Hornby and Bullock across Great Slave Lake eastward across the Barren Lands to Chesterfield Inlet in 1924-25. Fascinating story of suffering, starvation and survival with Hornby in the Barrens. Other, later, Hornby companions were less fortunate.

WHALLEY, George; *The Legend of John Hornby* 1962, 367p, appendices, index, 26 illustrations, 6 maps. A very well-researched, comprehensive book on the North and the life of John Hornby, including Hornby's many associations with George Douglas, Chritchell-Bullock, Edgar Christian and others.

WHITNEY, Caspar; *On Snow Shoes to the Barren Ground: 2800 Miles after Musk-oxen and Wood Bison.*

1896, 324p, profusely illustrated, 2 maps. A classic of the Hanbury and Pike era. Includes description of the author's hunting between Great Slave Lake and north to about 66 deg 45 min N lat in Mar-Apr 1895, with chapters on the Barren Ground caribou and musk ox; and comments throughout on the Indians and their customs.

WILSON, Clifford [Ed.]; *North of 55*: Canada from the 55th Parallel to the Pole. Toronto, 1954, numerous illustrations, several maps and diagrams. Sixteen chapters by different authors, covering a wide spectrum of topics, from the Fur Trade, Exploration, the Natives, to the Flora and Fauna. Writers include P. G. Downes, P. H. Godsell, G.W. Rowley, A.E. Porsild, Douglas Leechman and others.

WILSON, Clifford [Ed.]; *Northern Treasury: Selections from the Beaver*; Introduction by Leonard W. Brockington. Twenty-five selections from 1933 to 1954 from the Beaver magazine. Includes Guy Blanchet, James Bell, Thierry Mallet, Peter Freuchen and others.

photo credit Richard Irwin
I see your Arctic now.

The Arms of Arches

I have come to the outstretched arms of arches
Looked upward to the eyes of softness
And opened with hands of mornings the heavy doors
I have cried out in creeds and poetry
Knelt amongst the rose and amber
The warmth of wood
And risen with tears of voices
To touch the great vast stillness of prayer.

Yes Adagio, I see your arctic now
I see it, and am awed.
Everywhere is white
And distance
We live among diamonds
Fragile and perfect
And the sun who truly loves
This place of peace
Touches its warmth of red
Upon the arches of white
And rests the horizon of its silence
Upon the diamond distance
And you and I grow rose and amber
In the great vast prayer of stillness.

-Laurie